STORIES OF EMERGENCE

MOVING FROM ABSOLUTE TO AUTHENTIC

STORIES OF EMERGENCE

MOVING FROM ABSOLUTE TO AUTHENTIC

Mike Yaconelli, general editor

Spencer Burke

Todd Hunter

Tony Jones

Chris Seay

Chuck Smith, jr.

Jo-Ann Badley

James F. Engel

Frederica Mathewes-Green

Earl Creps

Brad Cecil

Jay Bakker

George R. Baum

Parush R. Parushev

Brian D. McLaren

GRAND RAPIDS, MICHIGAN 49530 USA

Stories of Emergence: Moving from Absolute to Authentic

Copyright © 2003 by Youth Specialties

EmergentYS books, 300 South Pierce Street., El Cajon, CA 92020, are published by Zondervan Publishing House, 300 Patterson Aveune Southeast, Grand Rapids, MI 49530

Library of Congress Cataloging-in-Publication Data

Stories of emergence : moving from absolute to authentic.

    p. cm.

  ISBN 0-310-25386-1 (pbk.)

  1. Christian biography--United States. 2. Postmodernism--Religious

aspects--Christianity. I. Youth Specialties (Organization)

  BR1702 .S76 2003

  277.3'083--dc21

                            2002156451

Unless otherwise indicated, all Scripture quotations are taken from the *Holy Bible: New International Version* (North American Edition). Copyright ©. 1973, 1978, 1984 by International Bible Society. Used by permission of Zondervan Publishing House.

Scripture quotations from **THE MESSAGE**. Copyright © by Eugene H. Peterson 1993, 1994, 1995. Used by permission of NavPress Publishing Group.

Edited by Vicki Newby
Designed by Proxy
Printed in the United States of America

03 04 05 06 07 / / 10 9 8 7 6 5 4 3

A NOTE FROM THE PUBLISHER

The emergentYS line was created in response to the rising interest of church leaders and growing numbers of Christians regarding the emerging church and culture—and the profound changes the church is now facing. The emergentYS line will address the complex issues of our world's ongoing cultural shifts and the impact this will have on the local church and its ministries.

The purpose of emergentYS is to provoke thought and conversation. This line of resources will help navigate the way we work through theological issues and open up discussion on topics that are essential for many people. Welcome to the conversation!

emergent
ys

ZONDERVAN™

GRAND RAPIDS, MICHIGAN 49530 USA

About the Authors

Owner of Youth Specialties, **Mike Yaconelli** is a popular speaker the world over. He pastors a small church in Yreka, California, with his wife, Karla. His latest books are *Messy Spirituality: Spirituality for the Rest of Us* (Zondervan) and *Dangerous Wonder: The Adventure of Childlike Faith* (NavPress).

Spencer Burke is creator and CEO of theooze.com. Spencer spent 20 years in paid ministry at Mariner's church in California. He's also a founding board member of Damah, an independent short-film festival committed to spiritual experiences in film. Spencer launched a new alternative to schooling called E-Trek, an experiential model that integrates real-time, real-life, peer-to-peer curriculum development and lifelong learning. An accomplished photographer, he has exhibited his work in galleries and taught at the university level. Spencer lives in a 1909 "beach shack" with his wife, Lisa, and their two children, in Newport Beach, California.

Todd Hunter is the former national director of Vineyard churches. For several years, he and his wife were actively involved in church planting with Vineyard and eventually moved into leadership. In November 2000, Todd finished his work with the Vineyard and left to plant a new church to reach postmoderns. Currently Todd is pursuing his vision to belong to a community of seekers, eager to follow Jesus and to learn what it really means to be the church for the sake of the world. In addition, he helps other church planters do the same by coaching emerging young leaders through a new, private, non-profit foundation called Allelon.

Tony Jones is minister to youth and young adults at the Colonial Church of Edina (Minnesota), author of *Postmodern Youth Ministry: Exploring Cultural Shift, Cultivating Authentic Community, Creating Holistic Connections* (Youth Specialties), and a senior fellow at Emergent. He lives with his wife, Julie, and their two children.

Highly regarded for his innovative thinking, **Chris Seay** is a leader in the emerging church discussion. He was the founding pastor of University Baptist Church in Waco, Texas—one of the earliest examples of generational church planting. Chris is now pastor of Ecclesia of Houston, Texas, and he's also author of *The Gospel According to Tony Soprano* (Relevant Books).

Chuck Smith, jr., is the founder of Capo Beach (California) Calvary Chapel and has served as its senior pastor for the last 27 years. Having come of age during the Jesus Movement, Chuck's passion is to create a niche for a new expression of Christianity within popular culture. He's author of *The End of the World...As We Know It*. He's the father of five and a grandfather as well.

Jo-Ann Badley is a biblical studies professor at Newman Theological College in Canada. As the self-proclaimed "token Protestant" on the otherwise Roman Catholic faculty, Jo-Ann also speaks at conferences in Canada and the U.S. Jo-Ann is finishing her doctorate in Pauline theology from the Toronto School of Theology, and enjoys reading, skiing, and spending time with her husband and two teenage daughters.

James F. Engel is a retired missions educator and consultant living in Minneapolis, Minnesota. His career objective has been to examine evangelical thinking, strategy, and practice in the light of biblical fidelity and demonstrated world impact. In the process he's drawn upon insights gained from nearly 40 years of ministry alongside thoughtful leaders in the Two-Thirds World. A well-known author, his most recent publication is coauthored with William A. Dyrness: *Changing the Mind of Missions: Where Have We Gone Wrong?*

Frederica Mathewes-Green is an active speaker and writer. She is a regular contributor to *Christianity Today, Focus on the Family-Citizen*, and *Touchstone*. A former feminist, Frederica has written several books and serves on the advisory and editorial boards of many groups and publications, including *Books & Culture, re:generation quarterly*, Common Ground Network for Life & Choice, and others. She has been interviewed on TV and radio shows including *PrimeTime Live*, CNN, MSNBC, *The 700 Club*, NPR, and many others. Frederica is one of the speakers with the *Los Angeles Times* Book Festival, Family Research Council, Cornerstone Festival, CareNet, and several other events.

Earl Creps is director of the doctor of ministry program and associate professor of leadership and spiritual renewal at Assemblies of God Theological Seminary in Springfield, Missouri. A former senior pastor, Earl is a frequent speaker at conventions, seminars, and retreats with special interests in communication, leadership training, and emerging church ministry.

Brad Cecil is pastor of Axess Fellowship, a postmodern outgrowth of Pantego Bible Church in Fort Worth, Texas. He's also a conference speaker, consultant, evangelist, and founder and president of Cecil Communication Group, which specializes in integrated marketing, media, and production services for organizations making a difference in the world. Brad is married to Suely and the father of four fantastic children. They make their home in Arlington, Texas.

Jay Bakker is the son of former televangelists Jim and Tammy Faye Bakker. After struggling through his teen years with drugs and alcohol, Jay began Revolution Ministries, which reaches out to inner-city youth in Atlanta. Jay is author of *Son of a Preacher Man* (Harper San Francisco) and has been featured in *Rolling Stone* magazine (September 16, 1999).

George R. Baum is one-half of the music group LOST AND FOUND. For nearly 15 years, he's played piano for the duo that continues to reinvent how Christian music is handled. Raised in the Lutheran church, George has returned to the Episcopal movement. With a life-changing story, he captivates readers with the lessons God taught him through his brother's death. George lives in Ohio with his wife and two daughters.

Parush R. Parushev (BS/MS, Institute of Precise Mechanics and Optics of Leningrad, Russia; PhD., St. Petersburg Technical University; MDiv. Southern Baptist Theological Seminary of Kentucky; PhD. abd, Fuller Theological Seminary) is native of Sofia, Bulgaria. He teaches theology, philosophy, and ethics. As a scientist and theologian, he has held a number of academic positions and has been a visiting and adjunct professor at several universities and seminaries in Europe. Currently he is the academic dean and director of applied theology of the International Baptist Theological Seminary of the European

Baptist Federation in Prague, Czech Republic. He has published a number of articles and books on science as well as articles on theology. He contributes regularly to EthicsDaily.com, an imprint of the Baptist Center for Ethics in the U.S. He's an ordained Baptist minister. Parush and his wife, Shaynah, have two children, Rumen and Emmanuel.

Brian D. McLaren is a sought-after speaker and highly respected author focusing on the church and the postmodern cultural shift surrounding it. He's founding pastor of Cedar Ridge Community Church, an innovative, nondenominational church in the Baltimore-Washington region. He's author of *The Church on the Other Side: Doing Ministry in the Postmodern Matrix, Finding Faith, A New Kind of Christian,* and *More Ready Than You Realize.* He's also a senior fellow with emergent (www.emergentvillage.org), a growing generative friendship of missional Christian leaders. Brian is married to Grace. They have four children.

CONTENTS

INTRODUCTION

The Illegitimate Church
Mike Yaconelli

I BEGAN MY WALK WITH JESUS 49 YEARS AGO. It's been an awkward walk, filled with stumbling, crawling, stopping. Over the years I have wandered away from Jesus only to find him finding me. I have doubted, I have struggled, I have turned my back on him, but he's never turned his back on me.

My faith may have sputtered and misfired, but in all these years my view of the Church has never changed. Notice it's Church with a capital C. The institutional church is another story. I have criticized, challenged, avoided, rejected, rebelled from, and ranted at the institutional church. I have been appalled, embarrassed, depressed, angry, frustrated, and grieved because of the godlessness of organized religion, the bureaucratic smothering of the institutional church, and the cultural worship of power and money gripping most denominations and church-related organizations.

But I've never lost my love for the Church, the glorious odd collection of unimpressive, ordinary, flawed people who make up the community of God, the body of Christ. Through all these years I have continued to find life in the unorganized, uninstitutional, irrelevant group of believers who are corporately trying to figure out who Jesus is and what it means to follow him in everyday life. I believe the Church has always been visible. It just gets lost in the glitz and glamour of whatever dazzling new ideas happen to be in the spotlight at the time. During the last 40 years, people have been captivated by the Jesus movement, the Calvary Chapel movement, the megachurch movement, a variety of Pentecostal movements, the Orthodox movement, the worship movement, and now the postmodern movement.

The longing beneath all these movements has always been the same—to find a place where people can worship God, learn about Jesus, share their lives in authentic community. One may emphasize integrity over authenticity or worship over orthodoxy, but all of these movements have tried to make the church real, to keep the church uncontaminated from the empty values of modern culture.

When I began to pastor Grace Community Church 16 years ago, I fell in with a rough crowd of people who wanted to be the Church, but voices around me questioned whether or not our church was really the Church. We didn't own any buildings. We didn't have committees, small groups, or denominational backing. We were a small group getting smaller. I was told I wasn't a pastor. I didn't have a seminary degree. I had been kicked out of both Bible colleges I had attended.

I began to question my call, question the validity of a small church that wasn't growing, question the value of a church with no programs, no buildings, and no paid staff. I was suffering from feelings of inadequacy and illegitimacy.

"Real" churches owned buildings, had paid properly educated staff, and, primarily did stuff. Church was about doing. This predominant activist model of church meant that the Church was all about attending, working, teaching, visiting, participating, performing, measuring, evangelizing, watching, committing, reading, memorizing, volunteering, joining.

Church was all about performance, and if you didn't perform, the church had no place for you. The minister was the mediator between the congregation and God, the hub of the church wheel. The minister had the vision and the church existed to fulfill his vision. Participation in church activities determined one's value. The sermons, teachings, activities, and publications were all about what Jesus wanted us to do, what God expected us to do, what the gospel commanded us to do—as seen through the eyes of the minister.

I don't recall (I'm older now, so my recollections may not be trustworthy) my soul being mentioned, except in reference to its final destination. I don't believe I ever heard the word *intimacy* connected to a relationship with Jesus. Numerous times I was encouraged to follow Jesus, witness for Jesus, serve Jesus, believe in Jesus, trust in Jesus, love Jesus, stay close to Jesus, and honor Jesus, but I was never encouraged to be with Jesus, experience Jesus, notice Jesus, enjoy Jesus, or savor Jesus.

The Illegitimacy of Legitimacy

By the age of 50 I was tired. I was beyond tired. I was exhausted. My fatigue was deep in my bones. My entire being ached for a God of rest, a God for whom friendship was enough, a God who was happy to be with me. I just wanted God to like me and to believe I was a legitimate minister of the gospel.

In desperation, after reading *In the Name of Jesus* by Henri Nouwen,[1] I found myself at the L'Arche community for the disabled, seeking what I didn't know. I met John and Tracey and Michael there, three seriously "handicapped" adults who in one week exposed the real handicapped person—me. While they frolicked in God's presence, they forced me to recognize the absence of frolicking in my own life. While they basked in the warmth of God's grace, I noticed how cold my heart had become because I connected the amount of God's grace I received with the quality of my performance. They could not perform, yet they ran in and out of the arms of Jesus with the full assurance they were unequivocally loved by God while I stood on the sidelines wondering whether I was loved by God.

At first I didn't notice any difference in me. One week at L'Arche wasn't enough time to see behavioral changes. In fact, much of what I experienced would take months and even years to bear fruit. But something had changed.

I noticed the changes first in my attitude toward the institutional church. I realized "the church of doing" was not the Church. I realized how life-smothering the modern church had become. I began to embrace my own illegitimacy.

I realized the modern-institutional-denominational church was permeated by values that are contradictory to the Church of Scripture. The very secular humanism the institutional church criticized pervaded the church structure, language, methodology, process, priorities, values, and vision. The "legitimate" church, the one that had convinced me of my illegitimacy, was becoming the illegitimate church, fully embracing the values of modernity.

What values? Let's take a look.

Efficiency. The Sunday morning services at most churches are models of efficiency. Notice how polished, orchestrated, and time-sensitive they have become. There are time deadlines to be met and parameters that must be respected. In seeker-sensitive churches especially, there is no room for spontaneity. Spontaneity takes too much time. It's too danger-ous if you want to leave on time. Sometimes you might see planned spontaneity, the illusion of spontaneity. Even in charismatic churches the "spontaneous" worship is controlled.

Today's modern service is orchestrated so nothing disturbing, uncom-fortable, controversial, or shocking occurs. The music is edited to elim-inate mediocre musicians or off-key singers. Solo numbers are assigned to the best. Prayer requests are screened or relegated to the bulletin where they can be carefully worded. Testimonies are screened to guarantee they won't make anyone uncomfortable or go on for too long. The sermon is inviolate. No interruptions are allowed, questions can't be asked, assumptions can't be challenged, disagreements can't be voiced.

Pretending. Church services have become conspiracies of pretending. The church has its own language. God-words permeate services, giving the impression that church is other-worldly. The minister pretends he has life figured out, and the congregation members pretend they don't have problems, well, maybe one here and there, mostly there.

Doing. The minister tells people what to do, and the people do it. Church is the reservoir of the uncomplicated. Jesus is the answer, the fixer, the problem solver, the protector. In other words, Jesus is the Chief Doer whose purpose is to do stuff for us, to satisfy our every need, want, and desire to prove to us that he is, in fact, God so we can go out and do stuff to prove we love God.

The Power of Being Real

I returned from L'Arche to my tiny, ordinary, mediocre church of 20 people. We relaxed and waited for God to show up instead of making him show up. My feelings of inadequacy faded away. Our church began a metamorphosis. Today we're the same tiny, ordinary, mediocre church…and yet…and yet…Jesus keeps surprising us with his presence each week.

Grace Community Church is no longer just a name. It's a description of the lingering fragrance of God's people.[2] Our little church is being the Church—we just didn't realize it for a while. As it turns out, we aren't doing a lot of things, which, I guess, the Church shouldn't be doing anyway.

We aren't editing our services. When someone who has difficulty staying on key wants to sing a song, the singer sings. Carol reads a call to worship—the words of a country song. It's difficult to know what it has to do with worship, but Carol knows. She is in tears, so we share in her moment of intimacy with God. Ken and Lisa interrupt the sermon because they don't understand what I'm talking about. Stuart interrupts to respectfully disagree with one of my conclusions. (It turns out he was correct.) Maria suggests she has a better illustration to end my sermon. (It was.) Sometimes the services are lengthy, sometimes short.

We don't talk about sin very often. In the 12 years since L'Arche, I may have talked about it twice. Do I believe in sin? Of course. Do I believe people are accountable to God for their sin? Absolutely. Do I believe it would be better if people didn't sin? Certainly. But the people who come to Grace Community Church know all about sin. Many of them have lived in it all their lives. It has destroyed their families, their incomes, their futures. They come to church to find out what to do about it. How do they escape the hold sin has on their lives? How do they find a way out of the addiction to sin? How can they find forgiveness and healing—and grace? We don't have to talk about sin. It's a given. What we're all longing for is good news.

We don't talk in propositions. We tell stories. Prayer requests are never routine in our church because there aren't any rules, just an unspoken assumption to tell the truth. Kathy began her request in tears, "I thought my drinking problem had been licked, I thought I was on the road to recovery, but I was wrong. These last couple of weeks my life has been a downward spiral of drugs and alcohol. Now I'm at the bottom emotionally. I've hurt and disappointed my daughter again. I'm on the brink of losing everything I have, and I need help. Please pray for me."

How could the congregation not be moved by her humility, her courage, and the desperation in her voice? A tiny woman began to pray. She had only been coming to our church for a couple of weeks, and we didn't know much about her. Hers was no ordinary prayer. There was power in her voice, authority, a depth of understanding that clearly communicated, "I know how to pray for you, Kathy, because I've prayed this prayer for me!"

Woven throughout her entreaties was her own story. "Lord, you know how you rescued me from 27 years of drinking and drugs. Yes, O God, I failed so many times, but you were right there to lift me up. Everyone else gave up on me, but you didn't and, Father, now I've been free of this addiction for many years. Lord, you've been my constant friend, constant companion, constant encourager." She went on to point out God's belief in us, his affection for those who have suffered, his transforming power to change those whom no one thought could change.

It was one of those special moments when you realize you've just had a glimpse of God himself. The entire congregation spontaneously broke into verbal affirmation and appreciation. The prayer had not only spoken to Kathy, it had ministered to everyone in the room. We corporately reaffirmed God's power and grace.

What happened? This woman's story empowered her prayer. And her story galvanized a room full of separate people into a unified body of pray-ers, able to lift up one person in fully united prayer.

Clearly story is central to how we understand the gospel.

The Power of Story

That's why we've decided to put together a collection of stories. For whatever reason, there seems to be a growing awareness that our stories are the workshop of our faith. Stories describe our interaction with God, the tale of God's presence or lack of it in our lives. Stories are the playground of our faith, the place where the logic of our beliefs gets tested by the illogical experiences of our lives, the workplace where our ideas about God run head on into the real God. Our stories are the testing ground where our perceived ideas about how God works come face to face with how God really works. Our stories are the daily journal of faith's complicatedness, the progress report of our journey with God, the roadmap of our attempts to follow Jesus in the twisted and complex jungle of reality. Our stories are our testimonies to how the historical God works in the present. Stories are the witness of our sightings of God, our periodic glimpses of him, and our daily frustration of trying to keep him in our sights, losing him in the busyness of our lives and then finding him again—or trying to find him.

Stories take our fantasies about God and bring them back down to earth where faith gets down and dirty, where our untested beliefs get tested, where our pretendings about God are unmasked, brought out into the open, and clash with the unpretending of the real God. Our stories about God are dangerous, unpredictable, wild, threatening, shocking, unprecedented, mysterious, illogical, raw, and discomforting.

But we must be honest. Stories are not facts. Unless we have photographic memories, we simply can't remember the exact details of our stories. Add to our poor memories the subconscious forces at work, and our stories end up revealing more than the precise details of what happened; they reveal the sum total of all the forces at work in our lives. In other words, what we remember—how we put it together—speaks volumes about who we are. Stories are not about what happened. They're about what's going on inside us. They're about the deep hiding places in us that show up and reveal not only us, but God's fingerprints on our lives. Ultimately what our stories describe is how God works in the manipulations and selectivity of our lives. We're hearing, in effect, the current mutations of God's grace in our own uniqueness.

Stories are always unfinished, partial, under construction, never over. What's great about stories is their incompleteness because that reminds us we're still learning, recognizing, and understanding—which reminds us how little we know. Stories are the agents of humility, because they make it clear God isn't done yet. Granted, the church has become good at manipulating stories to sound like they're complete and concrete examples of principles, promises, and formulas, but stories can't be captured and trapped and neither can God's truth. His truth is alive, ever racing in and out of our lives, always new, always fresh. Stories always remind us that the work of God is always ongoing and always changing and always revealing something new.

Stories are the most effective way to combine complicated and difficult-to-explain truth into simple, understandable bites of reality we can grasp. It's the difference between hearing a lecture on gravity complete with formulas and theories and watching someone jump off a desk. I may not understand the technical definition of gravity, but I understand gravity. Stories allow us to talk about what we know to explain what we don't know. It gives language to what we don't have the language for. Stories find a way to say what we can't say, to explain what we can't explain, and to reveal what we didn't know was there.

What makes stories so powerful is that they're easy to remember. Formulas and complicated diagrams are difficult, but stories (which are simply expressions of complicated diagrams) are much easier to remember. In fact we do more than remember stories; we internalize them. They leave a mark, a scar on our souls. Often stories end up residing in the deepest part of our souls where our tears and laughter live. Hidden in our hidden places, stories often show up when we least expect them, reminding us of truth we had forgotten or of truths we need at that moment to get through a difficult time or as illumination to help us make a difficult decision or as gentle graces from God to allow us to fall asleep or rest when we most need it.

This is a book that chronicles the new journeys of those who are trying to define and find Church, a book of stories. Each story is unique. Each story gives us a glimpse of Jesus as seen by a new generation of people who have uncovered his tracks in the dust and dead leaves of modernity. We will meet a group of people who have rediscovered the power of story, who see the gospel as story, who believe quite simply that Church is the place where we share our stories.

Are these the stories of the emerging postmodern church? I hope not. I hope, instead, they are the stories of an increasing number of people who are trying to be the Church at this moment knowing full well that the next moment the Church may look very different.

Questions

1. Mike describes being "appalled, embarrassed, depressed, angry, frustrated, and grieved" with the institutional church. What has your experience been like? What struggles, if any, do you have with the institutional church?

2. How often do you frolic in God's presence? What does frolicking with God look like? If you seldom or never frolic with God, how can you begin?

3. What would it feel like to be spontaneous in worship on Sunday mornings? To follow the Holy Spirit's leading? Is that scary is that for you and for others in your church?

4. Mike speaks of the power of our individual stories. Are there barriers at your church to sharing personal stories? What can you do to foster storytelling?

STORIES OF MINISTRY CRISIS

CHAPTER ONE

From the Third Floor to the Garage
Spencer Burke

I USED TO BE A PASTOR. More than that, I was a pastor at Mariners Church in Irvine, California—a bona fide megachurch with a 25-acre property and a $7.8 million budget.

Mariners is a great American success story. Founded in 1963 by a few families in a Newport Beach living room, the church has become one of the fastest growing congregations in the country. Each weekend, some 4,500 adults pass through its doors, with nearly 10,000 people attending its services and midweek activities. The church has everything a modern evangelical pastor could want. Great people, great programs, and great pay. The only problem is that I'm not a modern evangelical pastor.

Try as I might, I'm troubled by things like parking lot ministry. Helping well-dressed families in SUVs find the next available parking space isn't my spiritual gift. To be perfectly honest, I'm not even comfortable with some of the less sensational aspects of evangelicalism. Three-point sermons, four-law gospel presentations and 10-step discipleship programs have never rung true to me. And yet during my seminary education, to suggest anything else was heresy. To dare question my alma mater's premillennial, pretribulation doctrinal position, for instance, was to risk expulsion at worst and public humiliation at best. So like all the other students, I bought in. I read all the right books, went to all the right conferences, and said all the right things. For years I played by the rules and tried hard not to think about the lingering questions of my soul. Doubt, after all, is dangerous. Who knows where it might lead?

During my time at Mariners I eventually grew tired of keeping up appearances. After 18 years in ministry, the evangelical package started to unwrap. Swallowing my questions for the sake of the status quo no longer was a viable option. Sensing my anguish, the senior pastor presented me with the opportunity to start a Saturday night service—try new ideas and put a postmodern spin on the message. After deliberating long and hard, I decided to accept his offer.

The new service did well. I was glad to see students from my years as a youth pastor coming out on Saturday nights, now toting kids of their own. Even more gratifying, a whole new crop of people started attending—people who'd heard about the service from others in the community and had decided to come see for themselves.

I made the sermons narrative. To me, stories weren't just convenient illustrations, but sermons in themselves. And yet even with my new speaking style, I felt unsettled. Though I couldn't put my finger on it at the time, I knew something was wrong, as if the service were cross-wired. Some elements, like the music, were thoroughly modern; others, like my message, were quite different. Even more problematic, the more I identified with the new mindset of the congregation, the less connected I felt to the rest of the church's program.

Eventually I knew something had to give. When the pain of staying at Mariners began to seem worse than the pain of leaving, I submitted my resignation. I packed up my desk, loaded up my car, and drove home to my 700-square-foot beach shack. Five years later, here I sit.

Actually that's not quite true. I'm in the garage at the moment. I turned it into a makeshift office a year ago. My new digs aren't bad. A little crowded—and hot—but otherwise all right. If I want to strike up a conversation with my neighbors, I just have to smile and wave. Ditto for Travis, my postman. It's surreal. From a luxurious third-floor office—complete with a personal assistant and panoramic view—to an old weather-beaten garage. Who would have thought?

Since resigning at Mariners, the reasons I had to leave the professional pastorate have begun to crystallize in my mind. Although it's taken a few years, I've come to realize that my discontent was never with Mariners as a church, but contemporary Christianity as an institution.

Spiritual McCarthyism

One of the most significant issues for me is leadership. I'm not sure pastors should function like the chief executive officer of a large corporation. In a linear, analytical world, clear leadership lines are important to have—to know who's in charge and how decisions get made. If you've hung around the church for any amount of time, you've no doubt seen the business-style hierarchy in action: dozens of committees, a board of elders, a handful of pastoral staff members, and someone who has the final say. Enter the senior pastor.

In Christendom, we talk a lot about building the kingdom. Regrettably it often turns out to be the kingdom of man. Recently I've noticed more and more evidence of what I call *Spiritual McCarthyism*. It's what happens when the pastor-as-CEO model goes bad or when well-meaning people get too much power.

In today's evangelical world, one of the worst things you can be called is liberal. Challenge an accepted belief or confess doubt and you're the equivalent of a card-carrying communist. Brows furrow. Eyes narrow. Lips purse. Want to earn a place on the Colorado Springs…er, I mean, Hollywood black list? Admit your uncertainty about homosexuality as a biblically condemned sin. Want to be branded as a traitor in your own church? Admit your ambivalence about a denomination-defining symbol such as baptism.

And yet as I look at history, I'm struck by how many times the church has changed its mind on controversial issues. In antebellum America, for example, many Christians not only embraced but biblically defended slavery. No doubt they could quote passage after passage of Scripture supporting their rights to own African-Americans as property. Today, however, most Christians reject those arguments. In fact, most Americans—Christian or not—think slavery is morally reprehensible.

Similarly, at one time women were prevented from voting or owning property—a position the church heartily endorsed. Throughout history, Christians have been eager to shackle women both in and out of the church. Given a less-than-stellar track record, is it really so heretical to think that the evangelical church may be wrong about homosexuality as well? Isn't it wise to at least ask the what-if question from time to time, if for no other reason than to test our contemporary application of Scripture?

Not if you want to keep your reputation as a Bible-believing evangelical. Suggesting that homosexuality might not be as wrong as everyone thinks is a surefire way to get branded with a capital L.

I've wondered about communion. Growing up I heard about the dangers of "drinking the cup in an unworthy manner"—how the Lord's Supper was only for professing Christians. The proof text, of course, was always 1 Corinthians 11:29:"For anyone who eats and drinks without recognizing the body of the Lord eats and drinks judgment on himself." Since most Christians assume that all humanity is doomed apart from Christ, just how much would taking the elements affect a so-called unbeliever's fate? Would they go to hell twice? Or might it be a powerful first experience with the story of Christ? In a subculture where Spiritual McCarthyism has taken hold, those aren't good questions to ask.

Being blackballed by the local church is one thing, being blackballed by the evangelical community as a whole is quite another. In recent years, I've become increasingly concerned about the power certain evangelical personalities have over popular opinion. Call me crazy, but it seems like many of my church friends live on every word that proceeds from the mouths of the evangelical leaders of the world more than on every word that proceeds from the mouth of God. It isn't that what evangelical leaders say is right or wrong, it's just that so many people have stopped thinking for themselves—and those who haven't don't feel safe to express a dissenting opinion.

To me, Spiritual McCarthyism is about idolatry—about finding righteousness in something other than Christ. Every time I put on a mask for the sake of my reputation and career, I'm guilty of a sin far more serious than not believing whatever I'm supposed to believe. Rather than behaving as a son of God, I'm showing myself to be a slave to the law. I'm drawing my identity from what I do—or don't do—and expecting other people to do the same.

Jesus challenged the religious establishment in his day. He answered his critics with powerful, thought-provoking questions. He wasn't afraid to take on tough topics or discuss contentious issues. Spiritual McCarthyism, meanwhile, promotes exactly the opposite. It encourages people to orchestrate their lives to avoid censure and minimize risk. In short, it teaches people to live in fear—to put up and shut up. Fear, intimidation, and control shouldn't be the defining hallmarks of Christianity.

Spiritual Isolationism

At the time I left Mariners, I was troubled by the increasing separation I saw between evangelical churches and their communities. Everywhere I looked, Christian churches and parachurch organizations were pulling up stakes in major cities and heading for the suburbs. I remember driving author Os Guinness to the airport once and talking with him about the creation of the Christian ghetto—where real people with real problems are kept at arm's length. It's a fascinating idea, especially given the nature of Jesus' ministry.

On the surface, the shift to the suburbs would appear to be driven by the desire for expansion and less expensive land, but surely the move offers other benefits. It's simpler for families to arrive at church without having to step over a drunk or watch drug deals go down in the alley. Let's be honest: church in the city can be messy. Dealing with a homeless man who wanders into the service shouting expletives or cleaning up vomit from the back steps is a long way from parsing Greek verbs in seminary.

Spiritual McCarthyism no doubt also plays a role. If you believe that you alone have a lock on spiritual truth, cooperation with other religious groups and organizations becomes complicated. Even sharing facilities with the community can be challenging. The solution? The all-inclusive Christian package—a Christian Disneyland, of sorts, with everything from on-campus coffee shops to outdoor amphitheaters.

On the one hand, I admire the bold vision of megachurches. They're not afraid to announce $90 million building projects and ask God to provide. There's another part of me that's saddened by such prayers. Do we really need to have our own basketball courts and aerobics classes when a fabulous community recreation area sits across the street?

I heard about a megachurch that literally forced itself into a community. Many people in the area had serious objections to the amount of traffic and congestion the new facility would generate. Although the property wasn't zoned for a church and didn't have adequate access roads, the building committee was determined to proceed. After upsetting the residents and putting up a legal fight to get the project approved, the church finally opened its doors.

How do we process that kind of situation? At what point do we begin to teach the gospel? Is it once a facility is built and pews installed? Or should it happen throughout construction? And can a church claim to be part of the community if no one in the community wants anything to do with it?

Growing up, I believed in spiritual isolationism. I heard lots of people I respected talk about how important it was to come out of the world and be separate. Over time, however, I began to meet people who challenged that belief. As it turned out, a lot of my heroes weren't as separate as I once thought.

In 1977 I moved to Berkeley from a conservative Baptist church. I joined a Christian commune, took a vow of poverty, and set about learning everything I could about Jesus. I remember going to a local eatery one night with the man I'd asked to disciple me. We were just about to start doing a Bible study when he ordered a beer.

I was stunned. What? How could this happen?

That same year I was asked to photograph Chuck Colson. I was in his hotel room and noticed a pipe on the dresser. In the world where I grew up, you couldn't smoke and still be a Christian, so I asked him about it. Come to find out Colson had been given the pipe by the C. S. Lewis foundation. Lewis, too, had smoked! I was devastated. In just one after-noon, I lost two pillars of the faith.

Over time I met more and more people who didn't fit "the good Christian" stereotype. By their very lives, these people challenged me to stop speaking the code language of my youth—"Breaker, breaker. Smoky the Antichrist dead ahead"—and start engaging with the wider culture around me.

Throughout my last years in professional ministry, I felt a particular ten-sion between my life as an artist and my calling as a pastor. It was so bizarre to sip wine at a gallery opening of my photography on Saturday night then slap on a suit and preach Sunday morning. When the gallery folks found out I was a pastor, they were stunned. Likewise, my friends at church struggled to understand the arts community I belonged to. If the acquaintances I'd made in both these circles were to wind up in the same room, they wouldn't have anything to say to each other. That fact saddened me because I knew their spiritual journeys were painfully alike. Somehow though, boundaries had been drawn. Both sides had cloistered themselves away for so long, they no longer had the words— or even the desire—to communicate with each other.

Spiritual Darwinism

Permeating much of my experience in ministry was the underlying assumption that bigger is better. I can remember going to conferences and seeing a kind of Spiritual Darwinism at work. The people with a platform—the ones everyone wanted to hear and shake hands with— were always the guys from the big churches. Pastoral credibility had everything to do with how big a budget they had and how many worshipers came to the Sunday event. If a church decreased in size, one could only assume the pastor wasn't doing God's will and his books were destined for the discount rack.

While the church growth movement encouraged people to become more intentional about evangelism and to dream big dreams, it also fostered a kind of program-envy. The Christian community was quick to start shrink-wrapping strategies for success. As a pastor, I was expected to buy these ideas and implement them. There wasn't a lot of room to say, "Yeah, but…" to the latest hot book or video series. Looking back, I spent a good part of the 1980s and '90s going from conference to conference learning how to ride high on someone else's success.

As a seminary student, I quickly learned how important it was to evolve and advance up the food chain. You might start out as a youth pastor at a small church, but you wouldn't want to stall there. You'd want to keep moving into positions of greater responsibility and prominence. Work hard and be faithful and God would grow your ministry. If everything went well, someday you'd be the one on stage everyone wants to meet.

Simply shepherding a church wasn't enough. You wanted to have the *fastest growing congregation* or a similar label attached. It was survival of the fittest with a thin spiritual veneer.

It's funny though. At the time I didn't see any of these issues with clarity. My discontent with contemporary Christianity was something I felt more than understood. I didn't have words to communicate my concerns. Instead, I just had a deep sense of frustration and a gnawing sadness.

I went on a three-day silent retreat with Brennan Manning while I was still at Mariners. To my horror Brennan told us we should not read any books during this time—even the Bible. Instead we should only sit and let God speak to us. I went to Brennan telling him I felt like a phony. I even wrote a poem about it—how I was a mockingbird who didn't have any authentic voice. He nodded, and then asked why I was so angry with God.

Angry?

Was I angry?

I was. My wife, Lisa, and I had lost two kids early in pregnancy and nothing seemed to be going right. I was angry that God had robbed me of being a dad and mad that the evangelical program hadn't worked for me. I'd done everything I was supposed to—and this is what I got?

Brennan encouraged me to go back outside and meet Jesus. I was incensed. And yet as I sat there fuming, a strange thing happened. I felt like I could see Jesus standing there asking to come and be with me. In my anger, I refused. I could barely even look at him. Still, there he stood. When I finally relented, he sat down next to me and gently wrapped his arms around me. He didn't say anything; he just held me in my pain.

In that moment, I realized that God could handle severe honesty. Authenticity, in all its messiness, is not offensive to him. There is room for doubt and anger and confusion. There was room for the real me.

The Search for Authentic Expression

That experience seemed to mark a turning point in my faith. Shortly afterward, I stopped reading from the approved evangelical reading list and began to distance myself from the evangelical agenda. I discovered new authors and new voices at the bookstore—Thomas Merton, Henri Nouwen, and St. Teresa of Avila. The more I read, the more intrigued I became. Contemplative spirituality opened up a whole new way for me to understand and experience God. I was deeply moved by works like *The Cloud of Unknowing, The Dark Night of the Soul*, and *Wisdom of the Desert*.[1]

As my journey continued, I began to feel it might be time for me to leave professional ministry. I needed to find a place where I could safely unpack my faith and continue to ask *why?* A megachurch in the suburbs didn't seem to be that place. Within a few months, I clearly needed to follow my heart and resign—to cast myself on God's mercy and see where I ended up. I had no idea it would be in my own garage.

In many ways these last four years have been the most exciting in my ministry. Although I am not a professional pastor anymore, I'm still called to serve the church. By choosing to live out the questions in my heart, I'm able to dialogue with people in a way I never have before. I no longer consider myself a tour guide. I'm a fellow traveler and, as Robert Frost said, "That has made all the difference." [2]

In 1998, I started TheOoze.com. It's the kind of environment I've always yearned for as a Christian. Born out of my own personal need to have a safe place to ask questions and work through issues, it has grown into a thriving online community. Every day, people from all over the world, log on and dialogue about spirituality and life. The conversations there raise Spiritual McCarthyists' ire, but, using the Internet, we're able to enter into meaningful, honest discussions with each other.

People ask me about the name, TheOoze, what it means and how I chose it? It's actually a metaphor. The idea behind the name is that the various parts of the faith community are like mercury. At times we'll roll together; at times we'll roll apart. Try to touch the liquid or constrain it, and the substance will resist. Rather than force people to fall into line, an oozy community tolerates differences and treats people who hold opposing views with great dignity. To me, that's the essence of the emerging church.

I love the word *emerging*. As I look back at my own journey, I realize how much of a process it's been. I went through an adolescent phase where I could only define myself by who I wasn't, rather than by who I was. I'm happy to report that I've moved beyond that stage. Rather than only offering up criticism—as good and necessary as that may be—I'm also starting to take action. I'm making a conscious effort to orchestrate my life around a new set of priorities and to try new things.

For example, one of the ways I've tried to address the spiritual isolationism of my youth is to be more intentional about dialoguing with people who hold opposing points of view. I've already mentioned TheOoze, but I also sit on the board of the Damah Film Festival. The entries explore a variety of spiritual perspectives and come from independent filmmakers around the world. The jurors also come from a variety of traditions—everything from Judaism to the metaphysical. After years of having to separate my art from my spirituality, it's refreshing to see them come together. Even more exciting, I've been able to build significant friendships with people I never would have been exposed to as a professional pastor. Hollywood producers and directors even—the very people my upbringing taught me to avoid.

Although Spiritual Darwinism continues to plague the Christian community, I'm seeing positive signs. Through TheOoze I'm hearing more and more people question whether bigger is necessarily better. Each year TheOoze hosts a learning party called Soularize where members of our online community come together to share with each other. In 2001 we went out on a limb and offered a Native American potlatch—a spiritual ceremony of gift giving and grace giving—as part of the conference. An incredibly moving experience.

Under Spiritual Darwinism, the Native American voice has been all but lost. During Soularize we were able to reject the survival-of-the-fittest mentality and instead invite Native Americans to share with us in their own way. For Ray Levesque, a Tlingi who belongs to the 1,000 Tipis tribe, the conference was the first time area Native Americans who follow the teachings of Christ had been given the opportunity to address members of "the majority church" through their own cultural traditions.

More and more, my heart is about creating safe places for leaders to ask questions and to learn from each other. My passion is to network people and facilitate the learning process. In Etrek learning groups, for example, 14 learners and a facilitator meet, face-to-face and via phone conferences, over a period of nine months to explore topics chosen by the group. While guest authors, speakers, reading lists, and online learning tools are part of the program, the emphasis is on relational learning and peer-to-peer exchanges. The first groups have just started, so we'll see how they turn out.

I joke sometimes about TheOoze being a support group for crazy people in their garages—individuals who are struggling to fit into their churches and understand how cultural shift affects their faith. I laugh about it, but it's true. And you know what? It's needed. Knowing you're not the only one is wonderfully freeing.

No matter where you are in the process, I want to encourage you to continue on your journey. You're not the only crazy one out there. I can say with confidence, there are at least two of us.

Questions

1. Spencer experienced seminary as a place that squelched differing viewpoints. What has been your experience with seminary, Bible college, or the church?

2. Give some thought to your experiences with contemporary Christian culture. Have you been content? Discontent? What changes do you anticipate?

3. Spencer describes Spiritual McCarthyism as idolatry, "finding righteousness in something other than Christ." Do you agree or disagree with his assessment? How big a temptation is this in our culture?

4. Spencer says he believed in spiritual isolationism during his growing up years. What is your take on spiritual isolationism? Is it always bad?

5. Is it possible to practice Spiritual Darwinism with integrity? Does God want you to pursue "big"? If not, what does he want you to pursue? Explain your thinking.

6. What issues in your life do you need to hand over to God in "severe honesty," and with "authenticity, in all its messiness"? Are you willing to hand them over?

7. TheOoze and other organizations tolerate "differences and treats people who hold opposing views with great dignity." Is that helpful to the church? Threatening?

CHAPTER TWO

Entering the Conversation
Todd Hunter

I GOT INTO THE POSTMODERN CONVERSATION QUITE BY ACCIDENT. Demographically I'm a 46-year-old middle-class, university-educated, Protestant, white, male baby boomer. As Wendell Berry has written, "I...can only offer myself as such. I take no particular pride in my membership in this unfashionable group, nor do I consider myself in any way its spokesman. I do, however, ask you to note, dear reader, that this membership confers on me a certain usefulness in that it leaves me with no excuses and nobody to blame for my faults except myself." [1]

Psychographically I'm sure I would be pigeonholed as modern. I loved all the things now so popular to diss: *Leave It to Beaver*, *Ozzie & Harriet*, the Beach Boys, professional sports, and concrete, foundationalist *truth*. I was raised in an ultraliberal United Methodist church; converted into a "fundamentalist-light" church; experienced the full-blown, fire-hose blasting elements of the charismatic movement; sought to win others to Christ via crusades and the seeker movement; and drank deep from the well of church growth theory.

I have been a church planter since my early 20s and was the director of a new denomination—Vineyard USA. While minding my own business in that role, *the accident* happened.

Not That '70s Show!

For at least 20 years I have worked with young Christian leaders, especially church planters. Five years ago I noticed the current young leaders I was meeting with were not wrestling with the same issues I did when I was a rookie minister.

In the 1970s, our biggest battles were over whether it was appropriate to play soft rock music (now known as Christian adult contemporary) in church. It was thought to be bad when we brought in an acoustic guitar, worse when we plugged in an electric, but positively of the devil when we brought in drums. Drums, as the *adults* knew back then, were of the devil. "Why those sounds and beats come from Africa, don't you know?" (A horrible bit of racism—I say to my own shame, it took me years to see.) We were actually told that any song with a syncopated beat (a back-beat) was not of God. White, middle-class, evangelicals clapped on counts one and three, as in classical music. Only heathens from the dark jungles of the world accented and clapped on counts two and four. With all due respect to Chuck Berry and John Lennon, if it's got a backbeat, you *can't* use it! That's what we were told.

It all seems so trivial now, actually humorous. I sure don't mean to pick on anybody or blame anyone. Being guilty of misguided notions myself, I'm not about to slam my elders from the '70s. My wrongness, as it turns out, was a lot more substantial than honest ignorance about music. The problem with blind spots is that you don't know anything is there until it startles you by coming into view. This is precisely *the accident* that happened in young leaders meetings a few years ago.

A New Set of Questions

The contemporary Christian leaders I was dialoguing with were asking questions such as these:

"Is there truth?"

"How can one know it given our human fallibilities?"

"How certain can we be about truth?"

"Is all truth inherently good?"

"Are there ways of knowing truth beside the absolutist, foundationalist ways we were taught? If so, what does this mean for apologetics, theology, and church history?"

In addition to the questions about truth, there was nervous pessimism about church. These young leaders were wondering about issues of power, authority, and hierarchy on the one hand, and why the church seemed so impotent on the other hand. There seemed—for all the power to fight with and fight about—to be very little positive impact around. In fact, the power (charismatic or ecclesiastical) seemed only to be a source of control (stomping out creativity) or pain—inflicted during some version of discipline or culture wars.

When we were kids we joked around about the church and playfully criticized it. It was boring; we didn't like slow hymns and organ music. This is, by now, itself old boring news. I bring up this context because whatever the postmodern critique of the church ends up being, it will not merely sound like more of the same from the '60s or '70s. It doesn't sound like a cultural joke to ask (as many young people are): at the end of the day, is the church a net force for good on the earth or a force for (or at least enabling) wrongness—a spirit unlike Jesus or, at worst, evil?

As you can see, these are categorically different questions. They are huge and important when compared to styles of music. Most profoundly, the conversations always turned into implications: What are we to do differently given these struggles with truth and church now loosed in our culture? How do Scripture, the Spirit, and tradition inform this discussion so that we're proactive and not merely reactive?

Crash! The accident had happened! And it happened on my watch. I felt like the captain of a ship (my whole late-modern religious experience, not any one group) whose hull had run aground.

Resignation and Revision

Perhaps here I should answer a question I am often asked:" Why did you resign as the director of a well-known movement?" This aspect of my story may be instructive, because it included several streams of experience that made resigning a matter of conscience for me.

I wasn't upset at the Vineyard. Rather I have often used a metaphor to describe what felt to me to be a positive and exciting transition. I felt like a university president—spokesman, fundraiser and policy setter. Seeing the challenges of postmodernity, I wanted back into the classroom to do research and work with students, to figure out what it would mean to shape followers of Jesus into the people of God in the postmodern world.

My conscience often drives me. I am not a scholar or an original thinker. But I do think, and I read and interact with intelligent people. My position in the Vineyard afforded me access to bright ideas and learned people on a wide scale. I am sincerely grateful to the Vineyard organization for that. Looking back, three streams converged into a river that changed the shape of the intellectual and vocational riverbanks of my life.

First, for seven years I had the privilege of interacting with top leaders of denominations, many leading pastors in the country, some of the brightest sociologists of religion, key parachurch groups, and in-touch church consultants. When I took into account all of this learning, insight, and conversation, (a) everyone knew something was seriously flawed; (b) this perception was not often talked about with the rank and file; and (c) no consensus existed on what exactly was wrong (if you can't sharply frame the question, you can't get a clear answer) or what to do about whatever was wrong.

During this revisioning time, a key truism came back into my life: "Your systems are perfectly suited to yield the results you are now getting." Ouch! The realization that we were not in this state of affairs in spite of our best efforts but precisely because of them burst upon me like a foul refrigerator smell.

Second, I could see from several vantage points—my 25 years of experience and observation as a Christian, my travels around the world, many conversations with thoughtful people, and my work with pastors and planters—that Christendom (the social sense that the church is respected and a key player at society's table) as we have known it in the United States was beginning to lose its grip. Not to the degree it has in Europe or the United Kingdom, but noticeable to me. As I thought about this, I realized that almost everything I had been taught about church was based on the assumptions of Christendom. As my mom used to say: "What in tarnation are the implications of that?" What should we do differently in a setting where Christendom is disappearing?

Third, I discovered, as described above, the inroads of postmodernity along with the upset (in some) and excitement (in others) it was causing.

Seeing all this drove me to get back into the game. I don't mean that every denominational leader who sees what I have described and agrees with my analysis should do the same. I'm telling *my* story. My temperament, gifting, sense of calling, and desires all shaped my conscience in a way that made sense to me. To use a different metaphor, I felt compelled to get out of the CEO's office and into the backroom where research and development are done, where prototypes are created and risky creativity is celebrated.

I like the choice I've made.

A Resolute, Whole Life Story

The opportunity and necessity of responding to postmodernity has given me several great gifts. For the sake of space, I'll describe only one here. I rediscovered our *Story*.

In this process, I didn't lose any doctrine or facts, data or beliefs. Rather I better understood their meaning, their place. I came to see the devastation caused to our faith by reductionism and bullet-point approaches to apologetics and evangelism.

Postmodernism has made me into a postreductionist. I am grateful to Stanley Grenz and John Franke for some important vocabulary. *Beyond Foundationalism* reacquainted me with my desire to live in a story that began before creation in the eternal being of God, a story that is "universal in scope" and has "a historical consciousness, a futurist cast, an eternal focus, and is directed to a telos [an end]" of God's choosing.[2]

Everybody loves a good story, and God's is the best. More than that, Story has a more powerful impact on the postmodern imagination than mere propositions. I'm not saying that facts, beliefs, or data don't exist or that doctrinal formulations are unimportant. I'm speaking in relative terms. The most important issue I have in mind with the use of Story is to make sure that we're not giving reductionistic, context-less snippets about "how to go to heaven when you die" instead of the gospel according to Jesus (Mark 1:14-15), the gospel of the kingdom. Jesus' story is large and all encompassing. It holds the potential to become the organizing principle and force for a person's life.

In an article on *TheOoze* Web site (TheOoze.com), Eugene Peterson describes how Story has such influence: "The Bible is basically and overall a narrative, an immense, sprawling, capacious [capable of containing many things] narrative." Further, he says, "Story invites our participation…the Bible's honest stories respect our freedom; they don't manipulate us, don't force us, don't distract us from life. They show us a spacious world in which God creates and saves and blesses…these stories invite us in as participants in something larger than our sin-defined needs, into something truer than our culture-stunted ambitions."[3]

The effects of living in the wrong story are devastating to our churches. Countless thousands of well-intentioned pastors are left to try to disciple people who have no intention of ever seriously following Jesus or practicing their religion. The church is in grave trouble when discipleship (apprenticeship to Jesus) is viewed as extracurricular or optional.

This is the crucial point: people actually live from a sense of story, not from facts, data, bits of information, or bullet points to which they once gave mental assent. We live from our imaginations, shaped by and given passion by a story. Thinking again of Eugene Peterson, he perfectly captures my view and its practical, daily importance in his introduction to Matthew in *The Message*:

> The story of Jesus doesn't begin with Jesus. God had been at work for a long time. Salvation, which is the main business of Jesus, is an old business. Jesus is the coming together in final form of themes and energies and movements that had been set in motion before the foundation of the world.
>
> Matthew opens the New Testament by setting the local story of Jesus in its world historical context. He makes sure that as we read his account of the birth, life, death, and resurrection of Jesus, we see the connections with everything that has gone before…
>
> Better yet, Matthew tells the story in such a way that not only is everything previous to us completed in Jesus, we are completed in Jesus. Every day we wake up in the middle of something that is already going on, that has been going on

for a long time: genealogy and geology, history and culture, the cosmos—God. We are neither accidental nor incidental to the story. [From it] we get orientation, briefing, background, reassurance.

Matthew provides the comprehensive context by which we see all God's creation and salvation completed in Jesus, and all the parts of our lives—work, family, friends, memories, dreams—also completed in Jesus. Lacking such a context, we are in danger of seeing Jesus as a mere diversion from the [real concerns of life.] Nothing could be further from the truth.[4]

Perhaps you've heard the phrase *a storied* something—a storied sports franchise (the Yankees or the Lakers), a storied corporation (IBM or Microsoft), a storied orchestra (the London Philharmonic), or a storied dance troupe (the Rockettes or Russian Ballet).

Storied refers to something that has a celebrated, interesting, and important history. Normally this story is preserved and passed on in the daily environments of these organizations by decorations, photos, or clippings and by the old pros telling stories of yesteryears. These important and powerful symbols, icons, and storytellers draw others into the story.

Picture a young ballplayer as he walks into a famous locker room for the first time. As he does so, he feels his very best effort being drawn out in light of the *storied* atmosphere. Similarly, a young executive, seeing the boardroom where the business was built and the important decisions were made, feels the same awe and a tug on her brightest ideas and most creative solutions to current challenges. She naturally wants to fit with the best of her predecessors.

Likewise, the gospel of the Kingdom invites us into a large, all-encompassing story; the stories of Adam and Eve, Israel, and the church were always intended to be lived in. Living there is a huge privilege.[5] Choosing to live outside God's story has serious ramifications (a wasted life and hell come immediately to mind).[6]

Choosing to say yes to God and his story of interacting with a people on earth naturally involves our entire lives. When we're converted, we switch stories. We, like Michael Jordan when he decided to play NBA basketball again, naturally decide to do whatever it takes to fit our life into the new story. We work out, eat right, practice, and so on.

As I've processed afresh our Story, I have reenvisioned what it means to be a Christian, to be the church. Story reseated all the bits—Bible, salvation, substitution, community—back into their places with radically more powerful meanings. Context is everything. "Hit the bat" means one thing on a baseball diamond and quite another in the flying mammals exhibit of a zoo.

Salvation, as normally understood outside the context of the whole story (*say-a-prayer-so-that-when-you-die-you-can-go-to-heaven*), lacks the power to be compelling. The reductionist version was never right or true. Lacking the context of the story of God and his Kingdom, salvation became, in late modernity, just another consumer item that supposedly secured one's eternity.

The problem is the reductionist version of the gospel left out our actual life. Jesus became merely the Lamb, not the Lamb and Teacher for a new kind of life, in a new context: the Kingdom on earth and in heaven.

To help insure that I stay in a storied posture, I have begun to carry around in my pocket this resolution:

> I am going to apprentice myself to Jesus in order to learn to live in Ultimate Reality, the Ultimate Story—God and his kingdom. I intend to learn to do what Jesus did and say the things he said in his loving, confident, peaceful manner. I intend to be with him as his apprentice (through the Holy Spirit) doing the necessary and appropriate things (disciplines, means of grace) for apprehending this new kind of life. I do this for the sake of God, to work with him as he extends the benevolent rule and reign of his kingdom to others. I do not do this to earn or merit anything; it is my simple, but passionate (pearl of great price and treasure in the field), cooperation.

Where I've Landed

So, where have I landed, you ask? I'm not sure I have landed. It's more like *touching down gently* on the way to a proper landing.

I see postmodernity as just another worldview, coming in succession after premodernity and modernity. Not that the notions of truth and thinking are the same in each, and I know important issues are on the table, but each is still only a worldview. Each one contains inherent opportunities and threats with reference to Christianity.

Thus I don't want to be a faddish embracer of postmodernity or an unthinking critic of modernity. Neither do I want to be a wistful, naïve defender of modernity. Modernity on the whole has been no great friend of the church or the cause of Christ. Some bad things happened when God, the Bible, and the work of the Holy Spirit were brought before the courtroom of science, empiricism, and cynical rationalism. Modern philosophical romanticism and its equivalent reactions have not proven much better.

I'm happy to admit that modernity enabled great strides forward for humanity—freedom from the excesses of late medieval mysticism and wonderful inventions like airplanes and medicine among others. But, with reference to our faith, modernity taught us—to cite just two issues—to be suspicious of the Holy Spirit and suspicious of our sacred text. Scientific interpretations atomized the text (under the weight of finding logical, positivistic propositions) to the point that we lost all sense of story and our role as actors in it. The negative list could go on. (To be fair, we could list more improvements sponsored by the modern project in the medieval scene too.)

But that makes my point: *We are Christ-followers before we are a worldview.* Now hang in here. I'm trying to use my best thinking to let God and his Christ, the Holy Spirit, the Bible, and our whole family history (the Old Testament through to today), sit above and inform my worldview. I'm resisting letting an unexamined worldview shape my view of God and his project with humanity.

I can hear some say, "But this isn't possible." They're right in that it can't be done perfectly. But perfection can be a straw man. As a child, I used a lack of perfect ability to get out of all kinds of difficult or unpleasant tasks: washing dishes ("I always break some"); cleaning my room ("It's too hard. I don't know where to start"); mowing the lawn ("I might get eaten by the Weed Eater").

I'm trying to put this childish thinking away and to move toward clear thinking, even if we all stumble over context, perspective, and language. The context (a blistering, hot day), my perspective (mowing the lawn is stupid—it just grows back), and language ("Dad, this is, like, stupid, man!") never added up to the fact that the lawn, the mower, or my spanked butt weren't real.

So I peacefully grant the basic critique of modernity, and I think we all should. I also refuse the reactive, totally unnuanced view that says the only choice during this transition is between relativism (usually understood negatively as an excuse for or facilitator of sin and error) or absolute, positivistic truth. A little humility regarding our access of truth would do us all some good. If that gets me labeled *postmodern*, so be it. But I refuse to let postmodernity box me into a corner in which I cannot say or assert anything because of a reaction against the hubris of the modern project. Trust me, postmodernity has and will grow its own new forms of hubris. Modernity doesn't have a corner on some things.

What Is Truth?

Here is what I can say—at least for now—on the notion of truth: I feel most comfortable and responsible as a *critical realist*.

Three authors have shaped my thinking a great deal in this regard: University of Southern California professor of philosophy and theologian Dallas Willard, British historian and theologian N. T. Wright, and professor of philosophy John R. Searle from Berkeley.

I want to stay on the continuum of realism because it's apparent to me that a real world exists independent of my observation and interaction with it. Clearly a real world existed before humans, and thus it existed before our legitimate problems and concerns about perspective, context, and language. Searle puts it simply: "There is a way that things are…"[7]

I don't think I could believe in God if I didn't believe this was true. Believing in him, I also believe he has a kingdom—a rule and reign that created a world both independent of him and us. Here's a typical quote from Searle that informs my thinking:

> I regard the basic claim of external realism—that there exists a real world that is totally and absolutely independent of all our representations, all of our thoughts, feelings, opinions, language, discourse, texts, and so on—as so obvious, and indeed as such an essential condition of rationality, and even of intelligibility, that I am somewhat embarrassed to have to raise the question and to discuss the various challenges to this view. Why would anybody in his right mind wish to attack external realism?[8]

We may have limited access to this external world and thus the appropriate postmodern critique of the modern project. But the fact that I only have my perspective on something, that it exists only in a context, and that I am limited by my language in explaining it, these do not add up to, "There is nothing there, nothing real. There is not a way that things are." It just means we need a little "epistemological humility." Duh! This shouldn't be hard for anyone seriously pursuing the footsteps and heartbeats of the Master Jesus.

Humility is what brings us to the critical part of critical realism: we're always critical of our knowing about the external world. N. T. Wright explains critical realism as—

- Standing against the optimism of logical positivism and its assurance of unquestionable, fully certain, totally objective knowedge.
- Standing against naïve realism, that we know things automatically by common sense. This often devolves into belief in the guise of real knowledge.[9]

Rather than the above two options, Wright says critical realism is a way or process of knowing that acknowledges the reality of the thing known as something other than the knower (hence, realism), while also fully acknowledging that the only access we have to this reality lies along the spiraling path of the knower and the thing known (hence, critical).

In my terms, we're always critical of our present knowledge while simultaneously moving toward more perfect knowledge through the use of our critical faculties. Thus the phrase has a double meaning.

I am a working pastor and a coach for many current church plants. In those roles I have looked at the popular options for life and ministry. A critical realist approach is the best way to proceed. Done right, with a goodhearted spirit, it can go a long way in our theological and apologetic conversations.

God Is Not Stumped!

Finally, as a Christian, I want to actually believe in God and have confidence in his ability to deal with any worldview problem. Contrary to some hand-wringing Christian commentators, God is not stumped or in checkmate by postmodernity. He decidedly is not up in heaven, pacing on the golden streets, with his forehead in his hand mumbling: "Oh my self! What am I going to do? I didn't anticipate postmodernity! Hey, call all the angels; anyone up here know anything about deconstructionism, authorial intent, or language games? Anybody ever heard of Derrida, Rorty, or Foucault?"

No, our God is fully competent. He's worthy of our complete trust. He understands reality and the theories concerning it. He even knows facts! I couldn't be a Christian if I didn't believe this. But, believing it, I know that God raised up faithful spokespeople for himself in premodern and modern times, and he'll do the same in postmodernity. In fact, he already has. Some of the raised-up ones are now holding this book. It's your turn to play.

Coach Hunter says, "Into the game you go!"

Questions

1. How does the emerging church view "concrete, foundationalist truth"? Where is the place of such truth in today's doctrine? When might it be necessary to make assertions of truth? If there's an appropriate circumstance, how might postmodernity hinder you from making them?

2. What "accidents" are likely to occur in today's church such as Todd describes:"You don't know anything is there until it startles you by coming into view"?

3. From your frame of reference, answer Todd's question,"Is the church at the end of the day a net force for good on the earth or a force for wrongness"? Talk about your thoughts on this topic.

4. Todd was faced with a time of revisioning, a self-realization that the old way is no longer working. What should we do to reinvent the church and ourselves to continue the advance of God's kingdom?

5. How are Todd's concepts of story and biblical truth the same? Different?

6. What's your response to the resolution Todd carries in his pocket?

CHAPTER THREE

Toward a Missional Ministry
Tony Jones

I DRAGGED MYSELF INTO THE OFFICE RATHER LATE. It was Monday.

I should have taken the day off, considering the weekend we had. For the third year in a row, we had hosted a midwinter Christian concert in our sanctuary. Two years earlier we had a relatively unknown performer who charged $500, and we attracted about 300 people. The previous year we had a singer, now well-known, whose first album was taking off. She charged $1,500 and drew an audience of 600.

After that success, I decided to go for it. We booked a mid-sized band for $2,500 plus the cost of hotel rooms and meals. They appeared on the cover of *CCM Magazine* the same month I signed the contract. I promoted the heck out of that concert: press releases, posters sent to every church in the state, 50 free CDs to students, radio spots, and newspaper announcements.

The band was gracious but bedraggled when they arrived in town, exhausted from months on the road. We packed the house when over 1,000 students showed up. (At $5 per ticket, we covered our expenses and put some money into the 30-Hour Famine fund.) The band put on a decent show, but as we walked back to the dressing room we'd fashioned in the accounting office of the church, the lead singer told me, "We're more of a college band than a high school band. That really wasn't our crowd."

To add insult to injury, I arrived at the office late Monday morning to an email from a friend, saying the same band had played two nights later at another church's singles service…another church *about a mile from mine!* I happened to know the singles pastor there, so I gave him a call.

"Yeah," he told me, "someone from our group heard they were going to be in town, so we checked to see if they'd be available to play for us too."

"If you don't mind me asking, how much did you pay for them?" I asked.

"Five hundred dollars."

I was hot. I immediately called the band's manager. I tried not to shout into the phone, "You booked that band *two nights* after our show, in the *same town*, for *one-fifth* what we paid?!"

"It's a common practice," he replied, "Bands stack shows in cities like that all the time. We shouldn't have had them play in the same city; we usually try to space the venues by a hundred miles."

"But what about the cost? Is it negotiable? When I called you four months ago, you said they wouldn't play for less than $2,500."

"That's true for the first show in an area, but then the band tries to stack other shows in the area to make a little more cash."

"I thought we were all in the business of doing ministry," I protested naively." I thought that Christians were supposed to be up front and honest with each other."

Then this Nashville manager dropped the line that would finally cause my professional *metanoia*: "If you're going to be a concert promoter, you'll learn the ins and outs of the business."

Was it true? Had I become a concert promoter? I hung up the phone and reviewed my past four months. I had put in hundreds of hours on this concert, approving posters, negotiating with our church administrator about the use of the building, lobbying newspaper reporters to cover the show, lining up volunteers, selling tickets. The list goes on.

And to what end? When all the church buses pulled out late that Friday night, what spiritual impact did those 1,000 students receive? Probably little. I consoled myself: all those youth pastors thought Colonial Church was a great place that cared about youth ministry.

Let's be honest: I hoped all those youth pastors would think I was a hot shot, that I was on a first-name basis with Christian recording artists, that I could pack a room with a thousand kids. Could any of them do that? Wasn't I awesome?

Sick but true. When I looked deep inside, that was the motivation that had pushed me through the previous four months, at the cost of my relationships and to the detriment of my spiritual life.

What about the students at Colonial Church? Sure, they liked the concert, and they liked seeing their church full of kids. But they had basically been without a youth pastor for the last four months because I was otherwise consumed. *Who had they gone to with their troubles and questions?* I wondered. *Who had consoled, pastored, and guided them?* It hadn't been me, because I was a self-important concert promoter. Put that on the scales of eternal worth.

I sat at my desk feeling sick to my stomach and vowed to never promote another big concert. (You can hold me to that.) You can imagine how hollow all of the adulation in the following days seemed: "That concert was great!" "Thanks for all of the work you put into making that a success!" "It sure was great seeing this place so full of kids!"

Yuck.

In 1948, Bower and Jane Hawthorne joined 26 others to knock on doors and invite people to Colonial Church of Edina, Minnesota. It wasn't long before the fledgling congregation bought a plot of land and built a solid brick church that would become a cornerstone in the community.

In 1962, Colonial called a fiery young minister named Arthur Rouner, Jr. He was a unique mix of New England education and evangelical zeal. After a charismatic experience in the early 1970s, his faith and leadership took a turn, and missionary work in the 1980s influenced him yet again. As a result, Rouner led and preached as one possessed by the love of Jesus. His desire was to be a reconciling force—a bridge—between the mainline and evangelical branches of the Protestant church.

Bower and Jane Hawthorne were my grandparents, and Arthur Rouner was my pastor. While most of my peers grew up hearing either the evangelical emphasis on the doctrinal teachings of Paul or the mainline liberal emphasis on the teachings and example of Jesus, I grew up hearing about Jesus and who he wanted to be in my life. With a steady influence of Young Life staff and volunteers attending Colonial, developing the community was paramount, and openness to a diversity of doctrinal positions was highly valued.

I first articulated a call to ministry to my junior high pastor during seventh grade, sitting in his van in a McDonald's parking lot. I repeated it in ninth grade during a confirmation class, so throughout high school I was singled out for leadership positions by the youth staff. This affirmation was essential in my development. I learned relational ministry first hand. I spent many late nights with the youth staff, hearing their jokes, listening to them talk about relating the stories of Jesus to students. I felt like I had been allowed to see behind the Wizard of Oz's curtain, and I liked what I saw.

And, oh, the programs! We rented golf carts and held races in the church parking lot. We let 150 kids loose in a large shopping mall to look for a leader dressed up like Elvis and were escorted out by a less-than-happy security guard who was unafraid to let a few obscenities loose on our group. We once spent six hours setting up a miniature golf course throughout the church. (Six kids showed up; that's an hour of prep per kid!) Lock-in, lock-out, fall retreat, winter ski trip, spring retreat, summer mission trip, summer adventure trip, summer camp. That was the annual routine, and every camp and retreat had to have an awesome theme, replete with costumes for the talks, matching skits, and complimentary T-shirts. The time we spent planning the meetings!

After graduating from high school, I found college to be a significantly different experience. I matriculated at Dartmouth College in Hanover, New Hampshire, in 1986, knowing that I had to find a Christian community if my faith was going to survive the skeptical rigors of the Ivy League. Over the course of those four years, three things happened that spun my faith world off its axis and into the postmodern orbit.

First, I quickly became involved in Campus Crusade for Christ. My initial exposure was a freshman Bible study that about 25 guys—from all sorts of evangelical churches and parachurch organizations around the country—attended. By the time we graduated, about four of the guys were still practicing Christians. The overly relational, doctrineless faith they had received in high school couldn't carry them through fraternity rush and Philosophy 101. As time went on, I became involved with the leadership of Crusade at Dartmouth, but by my sophomore year, my questions about the efficacy of evangelizing the campus using only the Four Laws and Christian magicians drew increasing hostility from the Crusade staff. I simply could not abide the assumption that all the nonbelievers on campus needed was a simplistic set of propositional truths in order to be converted. Faith didn't seem that simple to me. Halfway through my sophomore year I was asked to leave Crusade.

Second, I was introduced to the work of Thomas Kuhn. Two of my favorite classes were in the Physics and Astronomy Department, and there I learned about the Copernican revolution and the church's response to it. In short, Nicolas Copernicus and Galileo Galilei led the scientific community in overthrowing the Ptolemaic earth-centered cosmology that had been in vogue for centuries. In examining this and other "paradigm shifts," Kuhn discovered that science changes by revolution, not by evolution, and in the years immediately following a revolution, the scientific community breaks into two camps: innovators of the new way versus defenders of the old way. During the Copernican Revolution and various other social, cultural, and scientific revolutions, the church has consistently taken the role of defender of the old. Being a part of such a conservative institution wasn't enticing for me.

Third, I was discipled by Edward Bradley. Bradley is a professor in the Classics Department at Dartmouth, a master of Western history, art, architecture, and at least seven languages—a true renaissance man. He values the life of the mind, enjoys the good life, and may be the best conversationalist I have ever met. Most significantly, he follows Christ as, in his words, a born-again Catholic. By that he doesn't mean born again in the evangelical sense but in the sense of one who has found and follows Jesus within the rites and rituals of the Roman Catholic tradition. Through many classes, several trips to Rome, and countless hockey games, he didn't disciple me in a traditional sense. Instead he exemplified a life of Christian integrity.

In the end, my faith survived the intellectual rigors of college, not because I was trained in any doctrine that saw me through, not because my faith had transcended doubt, and not because I avoided classes that would challenge it. While Colonial Church may not have invested in me the strongest sense of doctrine or a great training in prayer or Scripture, I knew beyond a shadow of a doubt that Jesus loves me. I knew the deep and abiding love of Christ intellectually because I had experienced it so many times in my community. That held me through college. During those years I understood Jude's words in verses 20-25:

> But you, beloved, *building yourselves up* on your most holy faith, praying in the Holy Spirit, *keep yourselves in* the love of God, waiting anxiously for the mercy of our Lord Jesus Christ to eternal life. And have mercy on some who are doubting; save others, by snatching them out of the fire; and on some have mercy with fear, hating even the garment polluted by the flesh. Now to *Him who is able to keep you* from stumbling, and to make you stand in the presence of His glory blameless with joy, to the only God our Savior, through Jesus Christ our Lord, be glory, majesty, dominion, and authority, before all time and now and forever. Amen.

That is, I both hold onto Jesus and am held by him.

When I graduated from Dartmouth, I was sure my future lay in sports casting, but God had other plans. Through a series of events, including a job offer at a church that was withdrawn two days later, I ended up in my brand new Ford Probe—packed to the ceiling—on my way to California. There, at Fuller Theological Seminary in Pasadena, Bob Guelich was the chair of the New Testament Department. Bob was an old family friend, and he offered me a spare bedroom—he said seminary was a great place to come to figure out what's next in life.

I was fortunate to take a couple classes from Bob before he tragically died of a heart attack. Despite the loss of my mentor, I decided to continue toward my M.Div. at Fuller. I was significantly influenced and mentored by three other professors:

Miroslav Volf, a Croatian, teaches and writes from a unique perspective: a charismatic evangelical with a real-life experience of oppression to inform the theology of hope he learned from Jürgen Moltmann at Tübingen. Volf shaped my theology, and when I visited him in Osijek, Croatia, in 1993, he shaped my worldview by pointing to the Serbian encampments on three sides of the city and telling me the story of the civil war that destroyed his country.

The late Jim McClendon was a baptist ("with a small 'b,'" he would say) theologian. His specialty was narrative theology, and through an independent study with him my senior year, I learned to find God's story in the lives of people. In McClendon's version of narrative theology, a person's life can exemplify a Christian doctrine, and my project was to discover how the doctrine of creation is explicated in the life of naturalist and Yosemite protector John Muir.

McClendon's wife, Nancey Murphy, had the most profound influence on me when I was at Fuller. A professor of philosophy of religion, Murphy opened to me the world of postmodern philosophy and articulated the intersection of faith and science. Those classes and chats over coffee were profoundly influential on me.

All the while, I was serving 15 hours a week as the junior high director at Pasadena Covenant Church (PCC). A midsize church, PCC is primarily Anglo, but our youth group attracted a mélange of white, Hispanic, and African-American kids. Looking back, I mainly feel horribly inadequate to minister in that context. We played games in the gym, we choked on marshmallows during Chubby Bunny, and I gave lots of talks on why not to have sex before marriage. During my last year there, I finally hit on an idea to use Fuller students to tutor the neighborhood kids in school work, which may have been the only ministry I did there that was contextually appropriate.

My next stop was in Manderson, South Dakota, with YouthWorks, a new youth missions organization. For two summers I lived in a little village consisting of one federal housing complex and a couple dozen outlying farms in the middle of the Pine Ridge Indian Reservation, the home of the Oglala Lakota Sioux. Every Sunday night, 65 students and leaders showed up in vans and buses, from a variety of churches. Every Saturday morning they pulled out with smiles on their faces about how much they had accomplished. In those days they painted houses, ran Kids Klubs, went to a powwow, heard a Lakota storyteller, and visited Wounded Knee.

While I directed them, mixed paint, changed tires, and massaged the diverse personalities on the tribal council, I tried to spend as much time as I could at Pinky's Store. Pinky is the unofficial mayor of Manderson in that she owns the only viable business in town. Her store isn't big, but it carries everything you need, and, more importantly, it's the place everyone swings through at least once a day.

Once I got the work crews off to their projects, I'd head over to Pinky's. At the little Formica table in the corner, I learned more about Lakota culture than I ever could have imagined, and I learned more about people, life, and friendship than at any school I've attended. In Lakota culture, you greet your elders with a soft handshake, you avoid eye contact, you speak softly, and you offer tobacco as a gift of welcome.

On many days, Pinky would say something to me like, "Jim Big Crow's wake is over at St. Agnes today. Buy a carton of Marlboros and bring them over there." Now, I didn't know Jim Big Crow, but Pinky knew what it would take for me to be accepted in Manderson.

"Laurie's husband skipped town last week," Pinky would say. "I gave her $10 for gas and told her it was from you. I added it to your tab."

By the end of my second summer in Manderson, something amazing had happened. I felt at home there. I don't say that lightly or flippantly. I was asked to serve on the security force of the biggest powwow of the summer. I was asked to pray at the beginning of important ceremonies. And at the Manderson Powwow in 1996, I was given a Lakota name (*Cankpe Opi Wakpala*—He Takes People into His Heart) and presented with the tribal flag.

What I learned in Manderson would fill a book, but primarily I discovered how to live missionally. I was more (or maybe less) than a missionary. I was not sent to Pine Ridge as a missionary, but as a program director. I didn't go as an evangelist, per se, but I did go as someone who carried the Good News with me. At the end of the summer, Shannon County was still the poorest county in the U.S., with the highest rates of alcoholism, diabetes, and unemployment. My presence didn't change that. But now, when I get a call from Aldean Twiss, the cook at Wounded Knee District School, or when A. V. Firethunder, a diesel mechanic in Pine Ridge, shows up at my door, I know that God used my presence there.

Al Roxburgh has written about doing ministry in *liminal* times—the thin times, the border times when we're in the midst of cultural change. He says that at those times—these times—we must live and minister missionally. Looking back, I think I was also in a *place* characterized by liminality. I was at a thin place between two cultures, and, by God's grace, I transcended my usual thickheadedness and lived with open ears and closed mouth. I learned everything I could about the Lakota culture—I ate their food ("puppy stew," Pinky said with a mischievous grin), drank way too much coffee, and rode in the backs of slightly unsafe pick-ups on highly unsafe roads.

At the liminal point between dominant Anglo culture and defeated Lakota culture, I learned some sensitivity. I saw behind the many inept programs of the Bureau of Indian Affairs, and I realized how little programs matter. In fact, programs often seemed like a way to avoid interpersonal relationships. I saw how a history of over 1,000 broken treaties—programs—had eroded trust. I sat with a table full of Indians at a restaurant in Rapid City and waited 30 minutes for a waitress to acknowledge our presence. I knew that sitting in Pinky's store, listening to stories and drinking coffee from a Styrofoam cup, had more impact than any program I could have developed. It was all about the coffee.

You'd think when I was offered the job as youth pastor of my home church in 1997, I would have learned that programs aren't the way to go. You'd think I might understand that relationships trump programs every time. Nope. Instead, I had stars in my eyes. I came in knowing that I could do it better than the last guy—more exotic mission trips, better T-shirts, faster golf carts.

Our junior high camps took off, 200 campers and another hundred on the waiting list. We had the best band, the most insane games, the biggest sound system. And we do have the best T-shirts.

Then we decided to pour our energies into the 30-Hour Famine, and we set the record for the most money ever raised by a single church.

Then we decided to put on big concerts…

The other day I got a CD in the mail containing an interview I did about a year ago. I told the interviewer that I didn't understand why, after three years at Colonial, I still didn't feel like a pastor. Then, two years ago, I got it. I wasn't a pastor. I was a program director, an event coordinator.

I wasn't alone. The profession of youth ministry came into its own only in the last half of the 20th century. Since the 1960s, as youth ministry became formalized as a profession, youth culture became *the* culture of the United States. Youth are the viewers that networks desire, the buyers that marketers envy, the listeners that CD producers dream of. Twelve-through 21-year-olds are studied, labeled, generalized, and stereotyped in an effort to get inside their heads to figure out what they might buy. Recently PBS aired an edition of *Frontline* entitled "The Merchants of Cool," which showed how clothing, game, and gadget manufacturers are so desperate to be in on the next fad that they dispatch highly paid young adult spies into high schools and colleges. This is big business.

Meanwhile, we youth pastors have also been trying to attract the attention of this age group. It's really not surprising, then, that we have resorted to tactics similar to Madison Avenue marketers, with a small fraction of their budgets. One of the latest schemes is to purchase a warehouse a couple miles from the church and outfit it with a massive sound system, video games, a café, and indoor basketball courts. The point of a facility like this is to pull in students by its outward trappings and then present them with the Good News.

It doesn't take much to deconstruct the philosophy of ministry behind such a façade, and it takes even less to show how incongruent the edifice complex behind such buildings is with the earthly ministry of Jesus. But it's hard to avoid developing a ministry that focuses on buildings, programs, and personalities. Senior pastors and elder boards aren't immune from the entertainment-driven youth culture. Just watch a week of the national evening news to view stories about "this enigmatic new generation that marketers relentlessly pursue"—you can almost hear the words coming out of Tom Brokaw's mouth.

Three thousand churches a year are going out of business, the elder board hears. Youth are the church of the future, so the implication is that if we miss the current trend of youth ministry, the church building will be up for sale in 15 years. With that kind of pressure, churches can hardly be blamed for going after young, energetic, good-looking, dynamic youth communicators. Then they throw money at the youth ministry and offer to build a new annex to keep that dynamic pastor, because his eyes are starting to wander.

I speak of what I know. Not that I'm young or dynamic or good looking. But I've watched thousands of youth pastors gather (I call them goatee conventions) to get an edge on the latest trick, the latest trend. They are, all in all, wonderful Christ-centered individuals. Many have forgone more lucrative careers to host all-nighters, drive church vans across the country, and sit through far too many committee meetings. These are good people, many of whom are realizing that the paradigm our profession is based on is a faulty one.

The problem for us is what confronted me as I hung up on that band manager and as I hung up on my misguided career detour as a concert promoter: what else is there? I had no other models, no other mentors available to me. Sure, I'd heard lots about people over programs and how the ultimate end of any event is relationship-building contact between students and Christ-centered adult leaders. But no one was showing me a better route into kids' hearts. I was in a quandary about how to proceed and wondered whether I should give up on youth ministry.

In the late 1990s, I got involved with a group called Young Leaders Network (then Terra Nova, now Emergent). It was a fluke, really. Already established for a couple years, YLN was putting on their first national conference in Glorieta, New Mexico. No one specialized in youth ministry. They were and are mostly church planters, many of whom were youth pastors tired of working within the structure of an established church. They knew of my interest in postmodern philosophy. I was over my head and intimidated, but I had a lot of respect for the leaders of this movement. One invitation led to another and another, and I guess I earned my place on that team.

Cross-pollination began to take place. I fought for the rights of some of us staying in established churches, trying to work within the system to be catalysts for change. Of course, systemic change is difficult, especially in an institution as inherently conservative as the church. But, I argued, great resources exist within the church and God cannot want us to consign so many churches that have done faithful work to the trash heap.

Meanwhile, all of these church planters modeled a missional life for me. During every meeting someone told a story of how the lease had run out on the church building or how his family couldn't afford the apartment anymore and moved in with friends or how the pastor's cell phone was the only phone number for the church. But the same person would tell about the church's skate park that just opened or the need to go to three services per week or the new art exhibition that had just opened at the church's café or hand out a copy of the church band's new CD made because someone gave $35,000 to open a recording studio.

This was not the comfortable suburban living I was used to. These men and women were indeed living on the edge of a new world, interacting with it in speech, art, and music. They were afraid of little—they seemed to me not unlike the courageous pioneers who settled the American West. And they had a Manifest Destiny attitude, too: God ordained and desires that we move boldly into this new territory and make the love of God known. Their lives were mission.[1]

After every meeting, I came back energized. Often I became frustrated with my fellow church staff members who seemed apathetic and pudgy compared to these edgy church planters, and I'm afraid I didn't hide my disgust well. My challenge was to become missional myself (as well as to be more forgiving of my coworkers). How could my life and my ministry become mission?

I've tried, in the past couple years, to make that transition. I admit I've had more failure than success. It's so easy when abandoning the program-driven model to embrace the small group/cell group model, the life-on-life mentoring model, the peer evangelism model, or whatever. They're all out there, and everywhere I go I'm asked two questions:

- What are you running? (What are your numbers?)
- What does your ministry look like? (What model do you use?)

The answer to the first question is easy: not enough.

I've pondered the second question, and I think we're a hybrid of four emphases (I'll avoid using the all-encompassing word *model*):

Pastoral Care. We try to be available for students' needs. Sometimes a student needs a friend to watch her softball game. Sometimes a guy needs someone to vent with about how angry he is at his dad. Sometimes a girl needs someone to talk to about the feelings of depression that are enveloping her like a thick fog. And sometimes, thankfully not too often, a student needs a friend to call the EMTs because he's just swallowed thirty-one Tylenol capsules.

Joan Metcalfe was the director of pastoral care at our church for 22 years, until she retired last year. In many ways, she's my model for this. Joan did a lot things you wouldn't consider "ministry." She knew where all the linens in the building were (we're still looking for some of them). She made sure the freezer was full of cookies for funeral receptions. She turned every mundane task into an opportunity to minister, to ask someone "How *are* you?" with that penetrating eye contact that means she *really* wants to know how you are. Plus she was at every hospital bedside, every graduation, every open house, every funeral. She *earned* titles like Mother Superior and Colonial's Grandma.

As far as I could tell, she never lost patience with a person's neediness. I cannot make the same claim…particularly about some junior high boys. Seriously, she modeled to me what it means to be in the business of caring for souls. I can't imagine a higher calling for a youth pastor or a better model for a youth ministry.

Theological Reflection. I am trained in theology, and I love theology. Early in my youth ministry I was frustrated that all this knowledge would be wasted if I stayed in there. But of course God used me in spite of my arrogance. Most of the dilemmas that face the teens with whom I work desperately need a little theological/philosophical/historical reflection. I'm not just talking about some Scripture from a Bible Promise Book that seems to vaguely speak to an issue, but something more sophisticated.

We're called to help our students see the events of this world, those that fill us with hope and those that fill us with despair, from this side of Easter—to view the world through an empty tomb. This isn't easy for you and me, and it's particularly difficult for a middle schooler or high schooler. I find the Socratic method works best, asking leading questions, answering questions with questions, and letting the disciples come to the biblical conclusion during their own journeys.

Contemplative Prayer. When I informally poll the students I work with, I find that most of them have no silence and little solitude in their lives. They're awakened by a clock radio, eat breakfast to morning television, drive to school with music, talk in the halls to friends, listen to teachers, wear headphones during passing time, listen to music on the way home, watch TV while they instant-message friends after school, eat dinner with the TV on, do homework with headphones on, and fall asleep with music playing. Their lives are filled with noise.

If I can give them some silence, I've done our students a great service. If they happen to hear God speaking in the "sound of sheer silence" (1 Kings 19:12, *NRSV*), all the better. Although he has communicated in the whirlwind, Yahweh more often has made himself known in the quiet places. The Christian tradition boasts a long line of contemplatives and mystics who have sought and found God by quieting themselves. Teaching this kind of quietude may be the most countercultural thing I do.

Intergenerational Community. I firmly believe that when Paul called the church the body of Christ he meant it. I don't think that he meant we constitute the body of Christ when we gather 10 high school boys for a small group. The practice of worship and the celebration of the sacraments requires the whole body in all of its gender/social/economic/racial diversity. Students need to be matriculated into the body, and not just on Youth Sunday. The 60-year-olds have a lot to learn from the students and vice versa.

Admittedly, our ministry is a mish-mash. It's tough to write a coherent mission statement for our ministry or to explain it to those who ask questions. Even though it's a fairly new experiment, I have found it so much more fulfilling than the old programmatic grind. Instead of being chewed up in that grinder, I'm energized. I'm sharing with students the very heart of our Christian faith, not trying to find a place that rents golf carts. That, at least, is a step in the right direction.

Questions

1. Tony's attempt to create the ultimate youth event came at a "cost to his relationships" and was to the "detriment of his own spiritual life." What in your life sidetracks you from your true passion to serve?

2. Are other people's perceptions of you a distraction that causes you to say yes to things you wouldn't otherwise? If yes, how can you change that?

3. Tony mentions people significant in his spiritual development. As you consider your own background, who has contributed to your journey of faith? Where do you see their ministry styles influencing yours?

4. What experiences have served to "spin your faith off its axis" as Tony encountered at Dartmouth? How did you respond?

5. In what way do you sense God calling you to live missionally where you are as Tony did among the Oglala Sioux? What encourages or discourages you from doing so?

6. Do you feel pressure to keep up with emerging trends among the next generation? How does cutting-edge ministry relate to stable church growth?

7. Tony offers four emphases for youth ministry at his church. How do these four rank as priorities in the ministry God has called you to? Is there a need for change?

CHAPTER FOUR

I Have Inherited the Faith of My Fathers

Chris Seay

MY GRANDFATHER, ROBERT Steele Baldwin (Papa), left a series of offbeat jobs like driving a Twinkie truck and selling vacuum cleaners at Sears to become an evangelist and eventually the pastor of Mangum Oaks Baptist Church in Houston. Mangum Oaks was a fledgling congregation with less than 10 people in 1966, but the church exploded in the following years. My grandfather, a gifted orator, told the story of faith with passion and biblical conviction. In the midst of this steady growth the church relocated to new facilities in a thriving area just outside Houston's 610 loop and added staff, including Edgar Martin Seay, a young college student turned music minister who quickly began to fancy the 16-year-old daughter of his new pastor. He married this teenage girl, who gave birth to me, James Christopher Seay, in 1971.

This is my heritage. It's where I come from. And despite the radical difference in my own ministry and lifestyle, I think of this brand of faith—what I call Revivalist Baptist—as the epicenter of my faith journey. At times I long for the security and nostalgia of this distant land. Mangum Oaks Baptist Church represents the homeland to me, a Mecca to all that it means to be revivalist. At times I long for the security and nostalgia of this distant land. I feel like Abraham—all at once loving my new adventure and missing the tranquility of my homeland. Yet the church has been swallowed by the emerging post-Christian urban landscape. Last year my grandfather's formerly thriving church, which he pastored for 28 years, held its last service in its 75,000-square-foot home. I'm no longer a wanderer turning my head toward home—there is no homeland. Instead I make a camp and hope to find a home. That is what this book is about: men and women looking for home, for a center that holds, for a tribe that becomes family. And like the Son of Man, we seek a place to lay our heads, theologically speaking.

As Doug Pagitt says, "Revivalism is about reigniting a latent faith that exists within people," but no flame—no familiarity with the story of God—exists to reignite. In its place is utter skepticism that a metanarrative exists.

I Am Now Postrevivalist

Within two generations the religious landscape of America and of my family has experienced a transmutation. Papa is the consummate 1950s evangelist, and Dad is a Swindoll-esque pastor. I thought I would lose my mind if I followed them into ministry. So I charted a new course but had no idea where I was going. Thankfully I embarked on this journey with their blessing. Please don't misunderstand me. My father and grandfather and I disagree, often vehemently, but they gave me this faith. The essentials (as stated in the Apostle's Creed) haven't changed. Almost everything else is up for grabs.

While studying at Baylor University, I accepted my first pastorate at the age of 18. If it was an exercise in my ability to assimilate into church culture, I failed. The odds were against me. During my second week on the job, I attended a seminary graduation where a former pastor of my church was speaking. The title of his message was "The Worst Church in the State of Texas." He told stories about a church with the meanest people you'll find outside of hell. These people had run off their last five pastors and were the reason many men leave the ministry. I felt like I had been kicked in the stomach as I realized I was the new pastor of the worst church in the state of Texas. And in the years that followed, I discovered this was no lie.

During this two-year stint in a church that felt more like a "fight to the death Baptist cage match." I discovered the beautiful objections to modernity articulated by a few French philosophers and the philosophy of generational characteristics. As I studied the writings of the few in the church that thrived on generational stratification, I resisted their approach. But they gave me a place to dialogue about the emerging evidence that my generation was post-Christian. The statistics at my university, Baylor, were undeniable. Out of 13,000 students only a couple thousand participated in any church or campus ministry activities. Even Waco, Texas, is a bastion of an emerging generation's mass exodus from the church.

The writings of Stanley Hauerwas led me to seek out an incarnation of biblical community. So I became the pastor of Bethel Heights Baptist Church, a small, rural, backwoods church where mealtime jokes about eating road kill were not just jokes. This family of faith taught me what it means to be community: they ate together, built one another's homes, shared everything, and laughed a lot.

As I experienced community I better understood the ranting of postmodern philosophers, my own generational observations, and my overwhelming sense that this required a missional response. So in January 1995, I started University Baptist Church in Waco with my friend David Crowder and a handful of musicians, an initial attempt at generational ministry.

University Baptist Church: Substance versus Style

I spent enough time surveying the land and mourning the state of my post-Christian peers. It was time to call them out—to establish a community of faith. I had no idea that this fresh way of articulating faith would connect with so many. The first year drew crowds anywhere between 25 and 1,000 people. We would gather to worship, and my sermons would flow out in a stream-of-consciousness style. Then we would close the service with a wonderful hymn of faith entitled "Hold My Hand" by Hootie and the Blowfish. Hootie was not the answer for my post-Christian peers, but his frat band melodies were a short-term remedy. I was finding the substantive shift was the real difference—the choice to allow Christianity to escape the confines of the Western worldview.

The Achilles' heel of generational ministry is the endless debate over all things subjective. Beauty is truly in the eye of the beholder. Listening to four men in silk shirts serenade me as they stroke the keys of their DX7 sounds like hell to me, but suburban boomers seemed to believe this is Nirvana (the state of bliss, not Kurt Cobain's band). In the late 1990s I did my best to convince them of their foolishness. I insulted their mullet hairstyles, mocked their booty-shaking pianist, and snubbed their band-in-a-box called the midi. They stood their ground seemingly undeterred. The wings of their hair grew fluffier, the pastels grew brighter, and soon the entire throng of miked vocalists began to shake their own booties. This was a war I couldn't win. People—large crowds of people—actually enjoyed this contemporary worship shenanigan. Who am I to rob them of such joy? So I gave up the culture wars. My battle between Eddie Vedder and Barry Manilow had ended. If they don't mind our worship sounding a bit like Dave Matthews or Coldplay, then theirs can relive the glory days of Neil Diamond with electronic drums and sequined shirts.

The transition I'm walking through now is much more about substance than style. I'm learning and growing with a group of peers known as Emergent. We gather to learn, grow, and sharpen one another, but mostly Emergent is about friendship. To learn more about this blossoming generative friendship, visit www.emergentvillage.org.

Pastor as Storyteller

I'm always learning to tell the whole story of God. I continually browse the physical and cultural landscape for the metaphor that will transform. I may find it in nature, an emerging band, or on HBO, but it's always there. Christ mastered the teaching methods of the Hebrews, as he traveled during his earthly ministry. He spoke with powerful idioms that left many puzzled, confused, and always questioning. His subversive stories had a similar effect, and one found that nothing was quite what it seemed. For instance, when Jesus told the parable of the lost sheep it has been said that he was responding to a popular Aramaic saying among the Pharisees that says "God rejoices when a sinner is condemned to hell." This was the popular understanding of God. Then Jesus tells a story that goes beyond destroying the heresy. It paints a picture of a God who would abandon everything to see this one person return to relationship with him.

Modern preaching has become the exact opposite. Our attempts to tie each passage off neatly into propositional statements that capture truth are backfiring and emerging generations see through the charade of our modern forms of exegesis. We are not simply autonomous knowers given the ability to decipher truth for others. Jesus understood that it's not only the truth that changes us, but also the *journey* of seeking truth.

In a world that is reembracing eastern thought like that of the Hebrews, let us follow Christ's example to become storytellers who bring

Scripture to life. This does not mean giving illustrations to support the propositions we have extracted from the text. It means telling the stories of our Bible from Genesis to the end. Mark Driscoll describes this dilemma:

> People are longing to connect in community as whole people while the church remains a goofy collection of individual minds with very bad pop music. Filmmakers have become the new preachers, telling spiritual parables to a listening world (i.e., *Seven, The Matrix, The Devil's Advocate*). Meanwhile, nutty, Christian, end-times-prophecy Kazinskis throw books on the shelves and films into the theaters trying to predict when we'll get off the postmodern roller coaster, while the lost try to figure out how to squeeze 10 minutes of semisanity in our breakneck, isolated, selfish, debt-ridden, sexually confused, lonely world temporarily propped up by Viagra and Prozac.[1]

Beyond Metanoia

Western Christianity has adopted the modern belief that "knowledge is power," that facts contain the muscle of Christianity. Therefore salvation is most often assessed by one's ability to regurgitate the propositions about Christ and faith. In theological terms this is called metanoia, the cognitive switch that turns in our head ushering us into salvation.

In the modern context, the church ignored biblical narrative and complexity, instead reducing the gospel to a set of propositions ("All you have to do is pray these statements, ask Jesus to come into your heart, and you're done"). But if that's all the gospel is, then all we need to do is wage a kind of air campaign, dropping propositions on individuals. As long as they buy the propositions, they're converted. We never really have to meet them or know them. Unfortunately, that's exactly what a lot of evangelism has resembled in the modern era. And it doesn't work anymore. We don't talk about the whole of life because—you've heard it before—"the supermarket does food, the politicians do politics, Hollywood does entertainment, and the church does the soul." We're left with a disembodied little chunk.

Historic Christianity—the entirety of God's story—must take the lead in our minds and hearts in this new century. If it does, we'll see some incredible things happen. But if we stick with a modern, Western Christianity, we're going nowhere. It's time to say, "No more." It's time to say, "The gospel is everything—the whole story of God for whole people." It's time to tell the truth.

Running in Circles

One of the primary reasons emerging generations are post-Christian is that the 20th-century church has focused on teaching that is logical and linear. These methods have been effective because the majority of the population has operated in a linear world. This is no longer true. Emerging generations employ multiple thinking styles as they process truth and information. If exposure to media, art, computers, and fractal imagery hardwires a young person's brain in a certain pattern, our attempts to communicate the gospel may fall on deaf ears—primarily because it's linear, not because of the content of our message. One of the reasons our churches tend to camp out in a book of the Bible like Romans, instead of exploring the rest of the canon is because it's a linear book. Thus, we have ignored Hebraic books like Ecclesiastes that employ a circular thinking style.

Thinking Styles

LINEAR   CIRCULAR   WEB

Let me encourage you to ponder the following three thinking styles and to consider the implications of limiting your method of communication to one of them.

You are likely to be familiar with the linear style. It's the form we teach seminarians to preach in and the one we use to explain the gospel. Our houses of worship are even built with straight lines. If you're trying to teach people who spend their lives in the church or in engineering schools, this is a perfect tool for the job. But it's not the only tool. If you only present the gospel in linear ways (the Four Spiritual Laws, the Roman Road, and nearly every way the church typically communicates the gospel) then you have preselected certain groups of people who will not respond simply because of the form of communication.

Circular modality of thinking is like what you find in the writings of King Solomon. In Ecclesiastes, the words of the teacher are carefully bound and are circular in thought. Song of Solomon employs a common Hebraic storytelling technique of starting the story at the beginning and progressing towards the middle of the book. In the last chapter you find the characters back at the beginning (the Shulammite is again an undeveloped young woman being protected by her brothers). Storytellers use this format in the movies like *Pulp Fiction, Momento*, and *American Beauty*.

The Web-oriented thinking style is connected, but with no predictable pattern. Like the book of Proverbs, it's a lesson in random or chaos thinking. We often describe people that think and speak this way as chasing rabbits or joke that they have attention deficit disorder. Thinking in nonlinear patterns is not dysfunctional. Visualize the way you surf the Web, and you'll see this thinking pattern. Each page that you see offers numerous options as does each succeeding page. Then imagine browsing the Internet in a linear format that offers one choice on each page. It would be an underwhelming experience. This is what many Web-oriented thinkers experience in our churches, sheer boredom with no intellectual or spiritual challenge. Isn't the essence of the gospel about bending, becoming all things to all people? This is an area that will require an immediate change in the emerging church. Please, consider the ways you communicate and the reasons your stories fail to connect.

Ecclesia

At Ecclesia, the church I began in Houston in 1999, we incorporate visuals into everything that we do. As I teach, large screens and monitors display photographs that visually accentuate the message. On the sides and behind me, artists simultaneously paint as we worship, sharing beauty and truth from God's story. Where some may react to a work of art as being "pretty," postmoderns often respond to art as being "true." I know a young lady who came to an understanding of the story of Christ completely through art. After graduating from art school, she traveled to Europe to see the great cathedrals. She was more disposed to Buddhism than Christianity. But the art in European churches made the gospel real to her. She chose to follow Christ based on the compelling story of Christ painted on church walls.

During the spring of 2001 our church hosted an art and music festival. Our members filled a gymnasium-sized room with all kinds of art, and outdoors we featured a stage where bands played everything from folk gospel to experimental punk all day. On hand were large portraits of Christ, jewelry, photography, sculptures, soaps, candies, and a tattoo artist who specializes in Hebrew tattoos from the Old Testament.

The people who were exposed to the story of Christ that day possess the most fascinating stories and perspectives you'll ever hear. I began to talk with a woman whom I had met once before. She's a tall lesbian woman with many tattoos and a spiritual hunger that was awakened by one of our Christian artists. I explained to her that I'm a pastor, but she didn't believe me. I told her I'm a church planter because the story of Christ has the power to change everything. I explained the gospel to her beginning with creation all the way to the gift of Christ. She hung on my every word. As we got to the death and resurrection of Christ and that he calls us to live in community together, she can hardly contain herself. In the same way a good Baptist would give a hearty amen, she exclaimed, "F*** yes!" over and over again.

The story of God hasn't lost its power or beauty. My friend is on a journey toward a real faith in Christ. It may be a journey that will take some time, so we must create new wineskins for new believers like her. She won't find a home in a Sunday school class or singles group. Finding a community that values her unique path and accepts real people will be essential. My own journey has brought me from the trappings of Baptist revivalism to a spiritual center in the arts district. I'm on the move, but, unlike Abraham, God has blessed me with the wisdom and encouragement of my fellow travelers. Emergent is a gathering of wanderers. We are searching for a home in an age of rapid transition. It's possible that a set of ideals will not ever bring us stability. Instead that assurance seems to be rooted in community, love, and relationship. Imagine that! A reformation built around mission and relationship instead of thoughts, systems, and ideals.

Thank you, Emergent.

Questions

1. In today's fast-changing world, many of us have lost our spiritual homeland, a place to lay our heads, theologically speaking. Where is your spiritual homeland? Does it still provide a place of refuge for you? If not, where do you find refuge?

2. The statistics offered regarding church attendance at Baylor University are staggering. What are some of the factors that have contributed to the exodus from the church? How can we reignite the flame of faith on our college campuses?

3. "Allowing Christianity to escape the confines of the western worldview" is what Chris credits as the impetus for growth at University Baptist Church in Waco. What do you think of his strategy?

4. Is substance or style more important in the emerging church? Should the balance be changed?

5. How can we incorporate the "journey of seeking truth" into Sunday morning worship?

6. Is your church prepared to embrace and challenge people to faith like those who attend Ecclesia? How can it become better equipped for the challenge?

CHAPTER FIVE

But Can We Get There from Here?
Chuck Smith, jr.

I ROSE FROM MY SEAT ON THE PLATFORM, smoothed my lapels, straightened my tie, and slowly approached the thick wooden pulpit. Carefully laying my large reference Bible next to my sermon notes, I cleared my throat and looked up, trying to make eye contact with as many people as possible. No one would be allowed to avert my gaze or dodge the heavenly thunder I was about to deliver.

Oh, I was good that day! Jonathan Edwards good. The kind of good that explores hidden pockets of repressed guilt lying in the cellars of our unconscious, then with deliberate harshness, drags them into the light of God's uncompromising purity. Men winced as they stared at the floor. Women wept quietly. Children were kept out of the sanctuary.

Old friends still talk—to my chagrin and humiliation—of that morning's sermon, "Sin in the Camp." I shouted, cajoled, and took emotional manipulation to a new low. As I reflect on those early days in Dana Point, California, I'm amazed at how cult-like we must have looked to visitors who had the misfortune of wandering into our church. We weren't interested in being the county's *biggest* church—which to us meant sacrificing quality for quantity. Instead we were going to be the *holiest* church, the epicenter of worldwide revival and the inspiration that would cause lost humanity to forsake evil. We were young, idealistic, ruthlessly fundamentalist, and—outside of our small circle—no one paid any attention to us.

If you knew us then, you wouldn't recognize us now.

Looking Back

In retrospect, I thank God for his gentle instruction and patient care. He gradually enlightened us to a better and more Christ-like church design. Step by step, he showed us the dysfunction of our theory and practice. Through his providence, God brought people our way who helped us envision a new church. Even to this day, our education is ongoing.

I cannot pinpoint the first breakthrough, but it occurred around the time John Wimber made a comment regarding my communication skills. He was curious why I preached the way I did and what I hoped to accomplish. I took my time explaining how people needed to feel the weight and wickedness of their sin. The pain and guilt would drive them to repentance. Then they would be motivated to live a holy life.

Wimber's response was short. "You're not changing anyone," he said. "You're just making them feel bad." The truth of his words emptied my lungs. I wanted to argue, proving that the Holy Spirit and Scripture confirmed my ministry of condemnation. But down to my bones I knew he was right. Lives weren't being changed. I had been beating God's sheep, not feeding them (as my dad would later comment). What kind of minister was I if my messages brought people down, sapped their strength, and made them feel inadequate and unworthy?

From then on I began to ask myself and God how each sermon could be used to give people wings, to lift their spirits, to energize them through God's grace. I had a new goal: people would leave each service feeling good, accepted by God and inspired to live in his love. I discovered and dispensed God's grace. I found that it was possible to extend mercy to people in the same way Jesus forgave prostitutes and adulterers.

Almost everyone in the church immediately responded to the change with relief and joy. I still lapsed into my old ways ("If you *really* loved God, then you would volunteer in the nursery!"), but most of the time I saw the value of concluding each message with grace rather than the law. The law tends to incapacitate people (see Romans 7), while grace enables and empowers them.

The transformation we were experiencing required us to review our prejudices and practices. We had to engage in the tricky business of distinguishing the negotiable from the nonnegotiable. We discovered the difference between cultural and theological compromise. We weren't free to rewrite Scripture, but we were free to reinterpret it and find new applications that were relevant to our immediate environment.

Transforming Influences

A number of people and events nudged me forward—and as I moved, so did our church. One life-changing experience came by way of studies in cultural anthropology. When I began reading *Cultural Anthropology*[1], my focus on the world I inhabited was suddenly clarified. Having been born and raised in a Pentecostal church, I was enculturated in a narrow worldview. The world of my subculture could not have been further from my high school culture if I had been a foreign exchange student.

Children from Pentecostal and fundamentalist homes often experience an upsetting feeling of being out of place in public settings. The activities that interest classmates are taboos within religious subcultures—drinking, partying, sexual exploits—and the values of the religious subculture—being "born again," "fellowship with the body," and the "rapture"—are unknown and bizarre-sounding to the larger culture.

Missionaries have the challenge of learning the language and culture of the people among whom they work. To be effective, they have to learn not only how to communicate with words, but to master all the symbolic gestures, signs, and customs that define a culture. A missionary who ignores culture not only sabotages communication, but also violates the incarnational model of Scripture in which God became one of us.

Perhaps it was while reading *Christianity in Culture*[2] that I realized the subculture of my youth had cut me off from mainstream culture. No wonder few people outside our church listened to us. We were unintelligible to them. It also occurred to me that to be effective among the baby boom generation, I would have to treat my connection with them as a cross-cultural adventure. In other words, I would have to learn their music, literature, interests, and customs to be able to communicate with them effectively. Sadly this revelation came to me in the late 1970s when I was already 30 years old.

What perplexes me is that Christians have known for 50 or 60 years how valuable cultural anthropology is to cross-cultural ministry, but we've never applied that knowledge here at home. We've assumed that we're the same culture as those around us, but we've failed to acknowledge our radically different worldviews; values; customs; and—in some cases—dress, speech, and mannerisms. We may live on the same street as our next-door neighbor, but when we talk about God, we sound like foreigners.

Why haven't we been encouraged to enter our neighbors' frame of reference, to see the world as they do, so we can communicate the truth of Jesus to them in a way that they can immediately understand? Why haven't we been more engaged in popular culture? Why have we allowed Christianity to be marginalized in North America?

For most of my life I was taught that too much interest in popular culture (the world) would result in a compromised faith. A number of normal activities (normal for everyone but religious kids) would lead to backsliding or even worse. But living under strict censorship and limited involvement with people my own age prevented me from knowing who these people were and what unmet needs might lead them to an interest in Jesus Christ and what he had to offer.

Through ongoing studies in communication and cultural anthropology, our church began to build bridges to our community and tear down the barriers that had kept people out. The way forward was not always clear to us—it never is to pioneers—and we made mistakes. But God has always been faithful to stay near us, guide our progress, and maintain our momentum. Jesus still patiently trains and leads his disciples.

Another influence on our church came through real-life encounters with the "heathens" among whom we lived and worked. We decided to engage with non-Christians in social situations without attempting to convert them. We discovered many good people outside the church eager to join us in almost any worthy cause. An honest reevaluation of our own environment revealed that there were plenty of bad people hiding within the church; people who justified their mean-spirited attitude towards anyone who disagreed with them; people who hid immoral hearts and deeds behind pious masks. We discovered how much we share in common with all humans. We also discovered that God was active outside the church—

without the help of our evangelistic programs.

One other influence that helped to reconfigure our church came by way of an innovative and prescient man, Jack Sims. Jack, whose business card described him as a horizon monitor, served as a consultant and visionary force in my life. Around 1978 *Cornerstone Magazine* published an article Jack wrote, "The Emerging Church of the '80s: Jesus Generation Christianity Comes of Age." The article was his attempt to look over the fence at the future and suggest a style of ministry he thought would successfully appeal to baby boomers. He made the following observations regarding the church of the 1980s:

- The church would place an emphasis on and have enthusiasm for contemporary music. He predicted there would be "a very strong desire for romantic, almost mystical, praise and worship music."

- The church would place a faithful emphasis on simple, practically applied Bible teaching.

- The basis for spiritual community would be the practice of agape love rather than doctrinal correctness or a shared spiritual experience.

- Sanctified prejudices would be replaced by biblical mandates.

- The churches would be marked by an intense commitment to evangelism.

- Young adults would be especially attracted to the new church because of its unique ability to appeal to their lifestyle and address their issues.

- The churches would place a new emphasis on praise and worship.

- The churches would manifest a climate of expectancy.

Sometime Later . . .

I sat at a lunch table one afternoon with Jack Sims and his friend, Joe. Jack asked me to explain what was happening in our church. I dipped into my past and recounted the social and theological events that produced fundamentalist Christianity. However, fundamentalism had aged and lost its cutting edge.

Out of the trunk of fundamentalism, a new branch grew called evangelicalism.[3] Like the wider cylinder of a telescope, evangelicalism stretched beyond fundamentalism, extending further into mainstream culture. Some of the old-timers adopted a siege mentality and entrenched themselves in fundamentalist subcultures or contracultures. Meanwhile, evangelicals, armed with a greater freedom to move about in public and a more generous attitude toward nonbelievers, went out to save the world.

But by the last two decades of the 20th century, evangelicalism was winding down. Many of the founders of its institutions were past retirement age. The culture around them had radically changed, but their perspective, strategies, and methods had not kept pace with those changes. No wonder many Christians began to think the hope for America was to return it to a 1950s Ozzie and Harriet world of moral and theological simplicity.

By now Jack's friend was scratching his head. He looked at me and asked, "Well then, what are *you*?"

I shot back, "I'm what's next!" Only now, many years later, do I realize how brash and arrogant I sounded. What I meant was that in the same way evangelicalism had telescoped out of fundamentalism, a new movement was going to emerge from evangelicalism that would cut a larger swath through mainstream culture. My desire was to belong to that new movement.

What comes next? We need to be constantly asking this question, because with the current speed of change in our society what comes next is constantly invading the present. That's the funny thing about horizons; they move as you move. As soon as we think we're on the cutting edge, some technological innovation or fashion statement has shoved us into yesterday's news.

Lots of Mistakes

By the late 1980s our church had moved from a small building in Dana Point to a remodeled bowling alley in Capistrano Beach, and we became Capo Beach Calvary. At this stage of our sociospiritual transition there were several concepts we knew pretty well:

- God was at work in the world.

- Many people were interested in Jesus Christ, the Bible, and spirituality but had a strong aversion to organized religion—symbolized by "church."

- Popular culture had undergone significant changes since the mid century that created new openings for Christian witness.

- A church would have to learn how to dialogue (rather than monologue) with popular culture if it wanted to get a foot in the door.

- God's presence in authentic worship was almost tangible, even for people who did not call themselves Christians.

- If we tried to be holy through dissociation from popular culture, we only succeeded in making the world think we were weird. If we sought first to build relationships with people, later they were likely to ask about our faith.

- Conversion to Jesus Christ was a Spirit-led *process* rather than an event that occurred as a result of an evangelistic promotion or script.

- Patience with people who embraced aberrant ideas or new age doctrines was often more effective in weaning them away from those beliefs than immediate and direct confrontation.

So how were we to make an impact on popular culture? One of our mistakes was thinking that attracting people to church meant we had to become glitzier, more Hollywood. This assumption puts a church in the awkward position of trying to match or outdo media productions like the Academy Awards ceremony every Sunday! We must have lights, movie screens, short plays, and coifed stage personalities as well as the best music. You can easily imagine the problems a church runs into when it assumes it must compete with the entertainment industry.

I'd like to suggest a problem that might not have occurred to you: the myth that all a church needs in order to increase its appeal to outsiders is a change in its forms. We think that sprucing up the old images and making superficial programmatic changes will result in busloads of new visitors to each of our churches.

A lot of churches are making this mistake right now. Under the banner of starting a Gen-X ministry or attracting baby busters and their younger siblings, many churches have taken steps they feel are bold and innovative. What they have done is merely changed the name of their youth group to something clever, brought in a praise band, added candles, and borrowed a bit from different liturgies. Some of these youth groups have also experimented with the arts, which tends to produce an aura of creativity and openness. A good ruse, actually.

Because clusters of evangelicals—and their children and grandchildren— live in most large communities in the United States, these youth groups with catchy names can potentially attract a lot of young consumers. Perhaps these young adults will bring friends who have no other evangelical influence in their lives. But we're deluding ourselves if we think we're making a dent in the huge population of post-boomers who are oblivious to our new format and who couldn't even fake interest in it.

Early on we made the mistake of thinking we could change the style of our service and expect the whole community to show up only to find out that when you improve the style of your ministry, the first people to arrive are Christians—bored with their former churches. Church shoppers are always looking for the latest and best entertainment.

The Missing Piece

To authentically connect with people who don't attend church requires us to make more than superficial changes in our external forms. We must undergo the painful process of changing our ways of thinking, our deep-set attitudes, and our mental paradigms. An old codger with a face-lift is still an old codger with a face-lift.

By now most Christians realize that we have an insider vocabulary—a specialized language that's difficult for people outside our religious subculture to understand. The problem goes deeper than the fact people don't understand what we mean by *sin, redemption, atonement,* and *sanctification.* The problem is that we ourselves have a faulty understanding of many words that freely fall from our lips. Our language is bound by old paradigms that no longer evoke the same reaction as when they were first introduced to mainstream culture. Our definitions of these terms are in desperate need of revision.

What is the *gospel* and what does it mean to be *born again?* We've heard a lot of talk about a *personal relationship* with *Jesus Christ*, but is that all there is to being a Christian according to the New Testament? We have abbreviated the essence of Christianity to short, simple formulas in order to sell it quickly in evangelistic rallies or cold-call pitches. But in doing so, we've diminished our biblical heritage and misrepresented the faith to ourselves and others.

Take, for example, the *gospel*. The evangelical summary of the gospel is that all humans have sinned, deserve hell, but through Jesus' death can be forgiven and can receive eternal life. In these terms, all a person has to do is accept Jesus as Lord and Savior and she or he will be saved. But according to the New Testament, the gospel is first of all Jesus Christ himself and the mystery of his divine-human nature (Romans 1:1-4). The gospel is about the kingdom of God (Matthew 4:23). There is much more to the gospel than the brief outline we find in evangelistic tracts. Salvation is both the complete transformation of a person's life and the result of that transformation. If people don't want their lives to be radically changed, then we should warn them of what it really means to be a Christian.

The difficulty people outside the church face when they experiment with visiting a church is not the *form* of the service—some people are even interested in historic forms of worship and devotion—but the *paradigms* that control our thinking. We tend to be unconscious of our prejudices, but those are the first red flags that wave in front of our guests. For example, a man who gives announcements or delivers a sermon and jokes about his wife's cooking, then goes on to generalize about all women, is considered rude. Even if the congregation laughs, people with sensibilities formed by popular culture will find it offensive, immoral, and abusive. What's revealed in such statements are old paradigms regarding family life or gender issues. In fact, our jokes often betray our old thinking.

Old paradigms include male hegemony, strict adherence to hierarchy, the assumption that biblical quotations end all arguments, anti-intellectualism (including hostility toward the sciences), holiness codified in external norms, anger toward people who disagree with us, judgmentalism, rejection of human cultures, narrow-minded dogmatism, the inability to acknowledge that a person may have a valid point or truth, ridiculing critics rather than treating them with respect and compassion, dependence on religious institutions for salvation, the notion that rational apologetics will once again be the most important force in evangelism, telling people what to believe rather than helping them form their own beliefs, and so on.

Fast-Forward to the Present

By the summer of 1993—30 years after the revolution—the North American landscape had been transformed. In a series of sermons I sought to define the word *postmodern* for our church and demonstrate fundamental changes in our thinking about reality, culture, religious systems, and each other. Though the term has recently suffered from misunderstanding and misuse, the phenomenon has still occurred, and our world has been forever altered. Some Christians are deathly afraid of the new world and stand at every gate to prevent its entrance. But you might as well stand in front of a tidal wave with your arms spread wide. Besides, the new era is not coming; it's here.

The challenge for Capo Beach Calvary isn't to become a postmodern church. I'm not convinced that it's possible or even desirable, and besides, we're too old. The challenge, as it's always been, is to get to know the dominant culture and to retool our church so that it can effectively be light and salt in a postmodern world. This, of course, means a reexamination of our current worldview, prejudices, and paradigms.

Some of the adaptations we have attempted so far include—

- Giving careful attention to film, television, music, and literature to take the pulse of popular culture.
- Developing a sensitivity regarding gender issues.
- Avoiding a public stance that would make people outside our church feel that we were not the place to go if their teenager were

to wrestle with the heartache of an unwanted pregnancy or substance abuse.

- Engaging in the social issues of our community and actively helping people in need.

- Involving lots of people in short-term missions trips that meet physical and spiritual needs.

- Seeking a common ground near the center of issues that have polarized Christians. The labels theological *liberal* and *conservative* have less significance today than in the past. They represent two responses to modernity that have outlived their usefulness. Now we're trying to learn as much as we can from as many people as possible who can help us grow in Christ and serve his interests in the world.

- Forming partnerships with other churches and organizations for meeting local and international needs; "subcontracting" with missionary and relief organizations that allow us hands-on participation.

- Addressing the dilemmas of our times, including the emptiness of hyper-consumption, our loss of identity, the advancement of relative truth, the spiritual questions raised in films and music, and so on.

- A greater engagement with the arts in order to enhance worship and enjoy the beauty and diversity of God's creation in the universe and also within humanity.

- Helping to plant churches led by young adults. I believe young Christians who are natives of postmodern popular culture have a better sense of what innovations are called for and greater freedom to create something new.

- Learning to avoid the kind of rigidity and oversimplification that reduces every issue to right or wrong and either/or. Moral action and decisions in our current context are always complex. To reduce them to simple *always* and *never* rules will fail the needs of people who really struggle to be good.

- Creating a greater sense of sacred space and sacred time so that God is more accessible to people. Modernity turned prayer into a machine-like function or formula rather than a harrowing encounter with the living God. People today need to taste and see; they need to experience the God for whom their soul hungers.

I suppose this backward glance makes it seem like we've come a long way. The pressure I constantly feel is that we haven't come far enough. The church is still playing catch-up with popular culture, and we will not have come far enough until we are a leading force in popular culture—if that ever happens again. Trying to sew new patches on our old garments isn't the way forward. We need new wardrobes. We need new souls, souls that are free to borrow and learn from Christian traditions, without being chained by them.

Early believers thought that Gentile converts had to become Jews before they could become Christians (Acts 15). It was a happy day for Gentiles when they learned they did not have to be circumcised to be saved. It will be another happy day when millions of people discover they can become Christians without becoming fundamentalists or evangelicals.

They will be what's next.

Questions

1. How do we convey God's judgment of sin without condemnation?

2. What are some of the reasons that the modern church has neglected popular culture? Why has the church been so slow to "enter in to our neighbors' frame of reference, to see the world as they do, so that we can communicate the truth of Jesus to them in a way that they can immediately understand"?

3. Why is it so tempting for a church to buy into Hollywood glitz in order to attract people? Have you found that to be effective?

4. Chuck makes a long list of paradigms on page 97-98 that serve to hinder people from outside the church from being able to engage in it. Which of these present the biggest obstacles to the church? How can we reinvent the paradigm?

5. As you consider the onslaught of postmodernism, are you poised to "stand at every gate to prevent its entrance" or to stand "in front of the tidal wave with your arms wide open"? What feelings stir in you as you think about this analogy?

STORIES OF WORLDVIEW CRISIS

CHAPTER SIX

Living as an Exile
Jo-Ann Badley

LET ME INTRODUCE MYSELF. I am a Baptist woman teaching biblical theology in a Roman Catholic theological college.

Am I displaced? No. I am at home.

But this is a postmodern world, and home isn't where it used to be.

Let me tell you my story. It isn't only *my* story; this story is also a story of God, and so I cannot tell it apart from *the* story of God. I will begin where I have found illumination in Scripture—this time in the book of Ezekiel.

I don't know if you find the stories of Ezekiel strange, but I do. Having Ezekiel for a neighbor would reduce property values. But in his strangeness, I'm drawn to his predicament.

Ezekiel was the prophet who revealed the word of Israel's God as Israel went through the most heart-wrenching and disorienting transition of her national life. He watched Israel go from being a nation with land, a king, political autonomy, and a temple to being a people with none of that. Even worse, a foreign king was now her head of government, and a foreign god given credit for Israel's demise.

Whether one were an Israelite left behind in the land or succumbed to Babylonian captivity, the situation raised enormous questions about what it meant to be the people of God in such a predicament. How could one look to the future? To simultaneously grieve what was lost and reframe your faith for the new situation must have seemed like an undoable task. How could the people of God be faithful to their traditions when the context was so changed? No wonder Ezekiel was strange; it was a strange time.

The book of Ezekiel and other writings from the Exile are helpful at this point in my history because, although he was a prophet living outside the land—in exile—he saw the vision of the glory of God moving out of the temple. The vision was a word of judgment, but also a word of hope. His vision reminded the exiles that although they were not at home, they were still living where God was. God would continue to be a glorious God who was with them, even where the conditions of life and worship were entirely different.

Ezekiel's strangeness reminds me that rethinking big changes might not look like I expect. I can't imagine what the modern equivalent to lying on your side for days on end while eating measured amounts of food cooked on cow's dung might look like, but I'm sure it would be unusual. And Israel's transition was certainly not painless. My experience of exile has also been marked by pain and unexpected grace.

The Land I Left

I come from a rich tradition of faithful Christian people. My grandfather on one side of the family was a lay Methodist preacher. He probably would have been a minister if he had money to pay for education. Instead he was an inept farmer who loved music and God and who was ridiculed because he would rather worship than farm on Sundays.

In 1925, years before I was born, the Methodist church joined in an ecumenical movement producing the United Church of Canada (UCC); it was a union between Presbyterians and Congregationalists. The UCC is the mainstay of the liberal Protestant tradition in Canada, and my mother's family members were staunch supporters of it.

My grandparents on the other side of the family were Mennonite immigrants. They came from Russia in the 1920s having lived through the First World War, the Russian revolution, a great famine, and Stalin. They lived their lives in gratitude for God's grace that had brought them through all those crises.

My father had left the Mennonite tradition of his parents, so I was raised in the UCC. We went to church. My mother taught Sunday school and cared for poor neighbors in our community. When she died of cancer, she died trusting God. My father served on church boards and his professional life was directed toward making the communities we lived in stronger: as a high school principal, he worked for school reform and athletic associations for rural students; as a government administrator, he provided the vision for community services for handicapped people in our province and later assisted Indian bands to take responsibility for the schools in their communities. I was raised to participate meaningfully to society, using my particular interests and abilities, and there were few restrictions about how that might look.

As a young person in the UCC, I made a commitment to God, but it was a commitment I did not hold to through my high school years. When I left home for university, I considered myself agnostic. At university I came into contact with a more vibrant form of Christian faith through InterVarsity Christian Fellowship. What particularly attracted me was the strong sense of community that existed among the students there as well as the ability of these Christians to articulate their faith clearly. I made a profession of faith as a young adult at that time and was immediately drawn to value the Scriptures, as this community did. The Scriptures hadn't been particularly significant to the faith tradition in which I was raised, and I expressed my disgust to my mother about this—I wasn't very charitable at first with my own history. I began to attend an evangelical church and was baptized.

Leaving the Land

Almost immediately I met with discrimination as a woman in the evangelical community, discrimination that the male evangelical leadership justified with Scripture. Strong gender differentiation colored all my relationships in this community, and it was a discrimination I had never encountered before in my life, at least in such blatant form. This was during the early 1970s and feminism was alive and well on my university campus; many of its themes made good sense to me. They fit with how I had been raised and with my expectations as a young woman in Canadian society. But the evangelical church I attended was completely out of step with this cultural situation. If exiled Israel was forced to leave the land behind, my experience was that the culture left the church behind; the culture was in transition, and the church was tenuously hanging on to old ways that no longer fit.

Let me recount a couple of early experiences that struck me at the time as completely absurd—experiences I could multiply tenfold from my years in evangelicalism.

I attended a Sunday school class with other young people from the university. The local InterVarsity worker had agreed to come and be our teacher. She was a competent Bible teacher and a wise, godly woman. However the church elders decided she could not be our teacher: we were adults, and she was a woman. Instead they appointed a young man who was not nearly as competent or as wise. Their decision made no sense to me, and they didn't seem at all attuned to the impact of their decision on the faith journey of the students involved.

I also remember, as a young woman of 20, being quite interested in the young men in the InterVarsity group. And while I was rarely asked out by the guys in that group, I did date young men I met in other settings. Eventually one of the Christian guys, a friend, came to me and said I shouldn't go out with non-Christian men. He gave me the unequally yoked rationale. But the men in the group were clearly attracted to women who didn't ask the questions I asked and were comfortable with the roles that the evangelical subculture gave to women. I was like a fish out of water; a square peg trying to fit in a round hole. I felt like the ugly duckling. I was faced with a choice: be unfaithful to myself or live my life on the margins of this faith community.

By the grace of God, I met and married a man who had strong faith convictions of his own and who has consistently valued the somewhat irregular gifts and interests of his wife. He came from an evangelical background, and we attended his church—the Christian and Missionary Alliance. I began to work as a professional woman, to live the life I had been raised to expect in a culture that expected me to participate. At work I was asked to assess management information systems, and at church I was asked to make cheesecake instead of brownies.

So what do you do when important parts of your life can't be integrated? One of my responses was to read everything I could find on the role of women in the church and the theological justification for differing positions. Since this was the 1970s, a lot was being written. In retrospect, I see this as *faith seeking understanding*, what I would now give as a good basic definition of theology. I was propelled to become a theologian, the very thing the evangelical subculture did not encourage a woman to become. In particular, I studied the biblical texts on the role of women because Scripture was such an important theological resource for my faith community. Reading and study were my most constructive responses.

My emotional responses were far less constructive; the wear and tear that comes from being the ugly duckling becomes more difficult to handle. I was alternately angry and depressed. Perhaps the greatest gifts to me in these years were several older women of faith who had been in ministry, however unacknowledged, who understood my dilemma. They accepted the person I was and nurtured me; they provided a place of refuge within the evangelical community.

After a while I could no longer make sense of the discussion about the role of women. The important essays were quite technical, and I needed the biblical languages—Hebrew and Greek—to make sense of them. My husband and I decided to go Regent College in Vancouver. My studies there opened up many nongender issues in biblical studies, all of which interested me and confirmed my focus on biblical studies. The study of the Scriptures has been the primary focal point of my intellectual life since then.

My experience at Regent also fed the ambiguity of my place in the church; the professors were divided about whether women should teach and be in church leadership. The debate was lively, both in class and out. The evangelical community continued to nurture both my love of the Scriptures and the dissonance that caused me to study hard.

Eventually my husband and I were no longer comfortable worshiping in the Alliance, and we began attending a Baptist church whose roots were in a liberal tradition that had undergone renewal. I remember weeping the first Sunday we attended. The ministers were robed and one of them was a woman who contributed to the service just like the others. We sang the hymn "This Is My Father's World," which I knew from my years growing up in the UCC. I felt as though I had come home. We have been in the Baptist Union of Western Canada (and affiliated churches) ever since.

After an eight-year hiatus in which I gave birth to my two girls and cared for them through their preschool years, taught Greek part-time at a local college, did some management consulting, and generally juggled a variety of interests, I returned to school to do doctoral work in biblical studies. I registered at an ecumenical theological consortium, the Toronto School of Theology at the University of Toronto.

At graduate school, I met a different subculture, the subculture of the academy. In my department this meant a largely male culture that focused on the historical study of the Bible. In this setting Scripture was not expected to be life-giving or to even have anything to do with modern life. Historical work pretends to set aside the concerns of this age in order to describe the events of another age. This conflicted with all my instincts and motivations for biblical studies. I was only interested in reading the Bible as a resource for the community of faith, and I was unwilling to divorce my academic work from my general purposes. After struggling for 20 years to hold Scripture and life together, to separate them now was counterproductive. Furthermore, I was suspicious of a subculture that did not attend to the motivations or implications of its work. I used the excuse that I was too old to willingly give time to other people's agendas, but this conflict of agenda was yet another marker on the way out of a modern land.

While I easily saw the limitations of modern historical study of the Bible, finding an alternative was more difficult. This time the grace of God came in the form of a Jesuit priest, my hermeneutics professor. He affirmed my questions and motivations. He also suggested a way of thinking that included my life experiences, affirmed the centrality of the story of God in Jesus Christ as the Scriptures bear witness to that story, and provided a framework for theological reasoning. That schema was postliberalism.

Postliberalism takes seriously that the task of theology is to restate faithfully the saving actions of our God and to think carefully about what that means for the community of faith in this new time. In particular the writings of Hans Frei articulate an evaluation of the modern academic biblical studies enterprise and gave me some guidance for constructing an alternate way to approach the biblical text.

Living as an Exile

As a Christian in Canada at the start of the 21st century, I see many parallels between my life and the experience of exiled Israel. In particular, the secularization of my society and the resulting devaluation of communities of faith is analogous. The church is like exiled Israel who found that her place in the world had changed: she had had control of her own affairs and voice in world affairs and now her life was dominated by someone else. Unlike Israel's exile, our process of secularization is not clearly marked by a hostile takeover. We are losing the land by way of a thousand little changes.

Simultaneously a growing plurality in Canadian society and in the world parallels the situation in which Israel found herself. Where her boundaries had once marked autonomous space, she now lived among aliens. Likewise I live surrounded by people whose life values and religious traditions are different from mine. I hear the words of God to Jeremiah, another exilic prophet, calling Israel to build houses and plant gardens among the aliens, to seek the welfare of the new place. But building and planting in a foreign place are hard tasks. The lament of the exilic Psalm is easier: "How can I sing the Lord's song in this foreign land?"

Then I think of Ezekiel. He was a priest. He knew the traditions of Israel well, and traditions are the soil of life. They bear witness to God's acts of salvation for us. I have studied the Scriptures long and hard. I bear witness in my life to God's acts of salvation on my behalf. I have known so much grace.

What do I count as this grace? First, a liberal heritage that gave me the skills and aptitude to live productively in the world. I face the realities of my culture and country with a confidence that God has not abandoned this place and with a sense of responsibility to participate in the broader world with charity and wisdom. This is my Father's world.

Second, evangelicalism has given me a vibrant faith, a love of the

Scriptures, and the motivation to study. This is grace even though that motivation came through pain.

Third, I count postliberalism as yet more grace, the gift of God in my doctoral work. It is an intellectual framework to reflect on what it means to live faithfully in my context.

Finally I receive as grace the fact that I was born a woman. God has taught me to love being an ugly duckling. In the final analysis, my deeper understanding of God came because of who I am. Being faithful to the particularity of my person opened the door to knowing God. And all of this is so unexpected. Just the other day a former student introduced me to her friend. She described me as "a woman Baptist theologian." Her friend thought there must be an oxymoron in that sentence somewhere. We laughed. God makes good jokes.

How do I think about my faith now? How have I re-formed it for the cultural land where I now live so that I am neither confined by forms that are no longer life-giving nor lost in a void where there is no truth, in a formlessness of a no-name spirituality? How can I be faithful yet flexible?

Again, I turn to Ezekiel. His final vision is of a temple, although it's difficult to picture and the vision doesn't seem to resemble the temple that was destroyed. But Ezekiel's temple is a holy place where the glory of God dwells, and from it comes living waters. The vision calls us to worship; it calls us to trust God for life. So, although the form changes, the person of God continues to be stable at its center, and God continues to offer life to those who worship there. Ezekiel doesn't live in the past, but he doesn't despise the things of the past. He lives in Babylon, but he doesn't forget the God of Israel. My world has changed—I cannot live in the forms of faith that served my grandparents and my parents—but I won't despise my heritage. I live in a world where Christian faith must be lived in new ways, but I do not want to forget God's faithfulness in Jesus Christ, made present through the Holy Spirit.

I offer you the metaphor of a tree. The essential shape of a tree comes from its trunk. I think of the trunk of my faith tree as the person of God, most clearly revealed in the life, death, and resurrection of Jesus. My tree is Christ-shaped.

The tree also has branches that get increasingly thin as you look toward the perimeter of the tree. These are the less clearly understood musings of faith, about which the church has argued for centuries. Different parts of the Christian church choose to live on different branches, and some branches are much thicker than others.

These days, I prefer to live near the center where things are sturdier, but that's because I have experienced what it is to be tossed in the wind by issues that can't be easily resolved. I'm older now, and the central things matter more. I refuse to focus on doctrinal peculiarities of subgroups, which seems to me to be living on a leaf. Autumn will eventually come, and the leaf will fall.

The tree doesn't look the same to everyone. The shape you see depends on who you are and where you stand. Are you a gardener? Are you in need of shade? Are you in the garden? Outside its walls?

What you see also depends on the season. Is it winter or spring?

What you see will depend on what direction the wind is blowing.

Clearly different people will see the tree in different ways.

I think of the Holy Spirit as the person of God who helps me to choose a wise place to sit in the tree and gives me the grace to be humble given the variety of branches and the expanse of green I see all around me.

How do I recognize my place? The criterion is the same as it has always been for all of God's people. Where God is, there is grace and there is life. In the words of Deuteronomy, God sets before us life and death, blessings and curses, and calls us to choose life, so that we and our descendents may live. Or, in the words of John, Jesus came that we might have life and have it more abundantly.

The means of life are the same as they have always been: prayer, worship, service, love of the Scriptures with their witness to the Triune God. I hear the challenge of Deuteronomy: love the Lord your God, obeying him and holding fast to him; for that means life to you and length of days in the land. I also hear the call of Wisdom in Proverbs, who promises life and favor from the Lord for those who find her. Paul reminds me that our God, who was also Abraham's God, is the God who gives life to the dead and calls into existence the things that do not exist. By grace, Sarah, though she was old, bore a son. The pregnancy was somewhat unexpected.

I don't find the loss of the modern world frightening. In many ways the postmodern world looks like the same dissonance I have always known, now appearing at the broader level of the culture. I do find frightening those who advocate postmodernity without humility, whether those advocates are in the church or in the world. An arrogance that assumes you know the truth, that you are like God, is always a danger, whether that arrogance is found in individuals or in communities.

In all this dislocation, I expect to experience unusual grace. My responsibility is to faithfulness so that I recognize grace even when it comes in unusual forms. Measured amounts of food cooked on cow's dung. Or a vision of a temple. Or a Jesuit priest. Or my female body. Laugh. God makes good jokes!

Questions

1. Jo-Ann recounts the experiences of Israel living in Babylonian captivity. She wonders on their behalf, "How could the people of God be faithful to their traditions when the context was so changed?" Are we in a similar position with the emerging church? How can we be faithful to our traditions when the context is so different?

2. Jo-Ann asks, "What do you do when important parts of your life can't be integrated?" What advice would you have given her?

3. Why do you think postliberalism became a philosophy that Jo-Ann was so eager to embrace?

4. In your opinion, does secularization of society continue to pose a threat to the church? Should we attempt to defend against it? What strategies should we use?

5. Jo-Ann paints a great metaphor of a faith tree. Where do you see yourself sitting in the tree? If you sense God wanting you to move, where should you move to? Explain why you think so.

6. Jo-Ann is frightened by people who "advocate postmodernity without humility" with an arrogance that assumes truth. Have you encountered anyone like that? If so, how did you handle the situation? How might you handle the situation now?

CHAPTER SEVEN

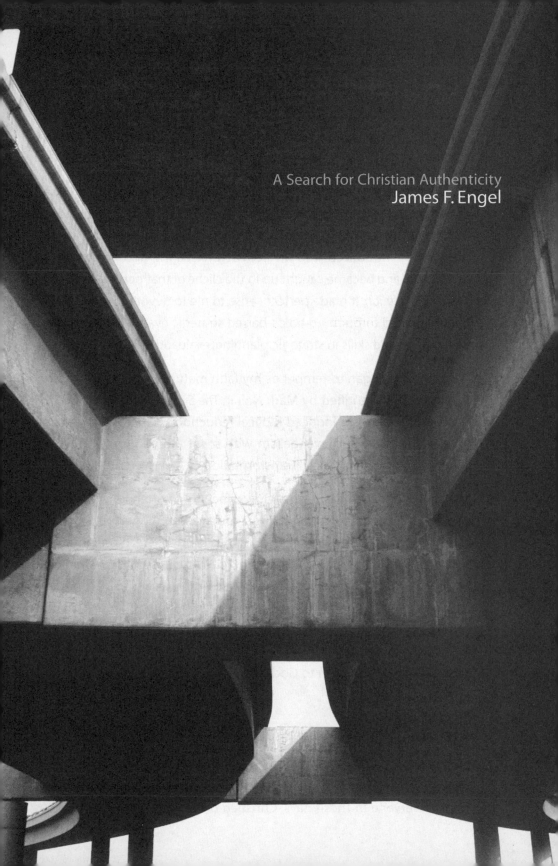

A Search for Christian Authenticity
James F. Engel

MY STORY BEGINS IN 1964 WHEN, as a churchgoer, I began to seek a faith that moved far beyond the bland, superficial Protestantism of my life to that point—a faith that could transform both my own life and the world in which I lived. I discovered the real Jesus Christ for the first time at age 31 in the midst of a successful university teaching and writing career in marketing and consumer research.

This, of course, was the heyday of modernism and the almost universal conviction that no problem is too great to be solved with human reasoning and initiative. Certainly that was the prevailing business worldview. I was quickly introduced into an activist Christianity also grounded in modernism and became caught up in the cliché of that period—*solution, spiritual revolution*. It made perfect sense to me to devote my life to winning the world through no-holds-barred strategic evangelism given my background and skills in strategic planning, evaluation, and marketing.

Soon my zeal began to temper as my faith matured. I discovered a disturbing reality identified by Mark Noll in *The Scandal of the Evangelical Mind*[1]—a modernism-induced biblical reductionism focusing primarily on personal piety and evangelism with scant attention given to personal discipleship and social transformation.

My life as a Christian has been a long, difficult, and often lonely pilgrimage to escape the contaminating influence of modernism on my Christian outlook. The major lessons I've learned are highlighted in these pages. Did this journey transform me into a postmodern? In many ways it has, but I prefer to describe myself simply as a Christian, or perhaps as a premodern, a fellow struggler attempting to help myself and others to return to our historic pilgrim heritage dedicated to bringing "all aspects of life—political, social, cultural, economic, artistic, or ecclesiastical—into subjection to God."[2]

My Life before Christ Became a Living Reality

Like so many people in the United States, I was raised in the church and participated in Sunday school and youth groups in the 1940s and '50s. Nearly everyone in those days, Christian or not, accepted the need to live moral lives following what we understood to be the Golden Rule. After all, these were the values accepted by American society even though the Christian roots had largely been cut. Christianity, however, was little more than a poorly understood ethical code for me and not a living reality.

My father was a preacher's kid who rejected his faith and deserted my mother and me after service during World War II. As a result, I was raised by my mother, a Christian, living with deep inner uncertainties and fears dating back to her childhood. Although she did her best, she compensated for her own frustrations by prodding me to be the best at everything I did. What this did was to put an already entrepreneurial kid on the track of unrelenting achievement, the highly valued central motivation in modernism that still plagues me at times even in retirement.

From early in life I have been driven by a desire for success. After all, this was the road to the top. When I received my doctorate in business In 1960, my goal was to teach at the best business school in the United States. I set my sights on the University of Michigan Graduate School of Business and started at that great university on what was to be a fast track to success. Later I moved into an even more rewarding professorship at Ohio State University where I taught for nine years.

During those years I became recognized as a leading marketing authority. My books on promotional strategy and consumer behavior soon became standards worldwide. I was acknowledged as the founder of the field of consumer research, which I and a few other colleagues launched in the 1960s.

In short, I was king of the hill—a poster person for modernism—the successful achievement-driven entrepreneur. I had a beautiful, gracious wife, Sharon, and twin daughters. We continued a sincere but passive involvement in church, following patterns established in our childhood. My life appeared to be ideal, but by the time I was in my early 30s life began to lose its luster. Both Sharon and I felt a real dissatisfaction that peaked during six months in New York City in 1964 when I was privileged to be a faculty visitor in one of the world's top advertising agencies.

One Sunday we attended the Marble Collegiate Church and sensed something entirely fresh. We meet people whose vitality was contagious. From there we set out on a pilgrimage of several months that led us to the life-changing discovery of what Christianity is all about. This was a radical new beginning for both of us. We wanted to make our lives count for Christ.

The New Kid on the Evangelical Block

After this life-changing experience, I continued as a professor at Ohio State until 1972. While my motivation to achieve remained largely intact, the direction took a dramatic shift as Christ became increasingly real and vital. I became involved both nationally and at Ohio State in campus evangelism—a significant opportunity. In that capacity I traveled the United States frequently in a growing ministry to motivate Christian faculty to become involved meaningfully in campus outreach. I learned about trench evangelism through days that often began at breakfast meetings and ended past midnight. In other words, I became a card-carrying evangelical by this single-minded lifestyle.

Although I continued to be active as a recognized marketing author into the 1990s, my career took a turn when I went to the Wheaton College Graduate School in 1972 as a visiting scholar on a one-year leave to study theology. Much to my surprise, God led me to assume a leadership role in Wheaton's pioneering Graduate Communications Program, a role that lasted for 18 years. Later I was called to my last position at Eastern University in Philadelphia in 1990 where David Fraser, Jane Overstreet, and I founded the Center for Organizational Excellence dedicated to preparing much-needed leadership development curricula for the Two-Thirds World. This soon was followed by the formation of Development Associates International, a recognized worldwide leadership development agency.

Unfortunately, my achievement motivation seemed to survive intact, and I became an equal success in the Christian arena through my writings, teaching, and consulting on ministry effectiveness. Once again I was a poster person for modernism. I loved this spotlight, but my own inner struggles continued—even magnified. Matters came to a head in the early 1980s when I found myself outwardly successful but inwardly bankrupt. Through an invaluable period of counseling, reflection, and receiving help from others, I found myself on an all-new pilgrimage, having my outlook on life and ministry reshaped, a process that continues today.

My Emancipation from Modernism

The enlightenment leading to modernism has been beneficial in many ways, especially in releasing the Christian mind from its bondage lasting hundreds of years during the Middle Ages. Indeed, it created and provided the climate in which I could use my gifts in an entrepreneurial way to the glory of God. I often have challenged the status quo through my teaching and writings and have triggered many to rethink their directions in life and ministry.

My life crisis in the 1980s, however, sharply magnified a process that had begun years earlier as I began to use the lens of Scripture, the history of Christian witness, and theology to evaluate the priorities and practices of life and ministry. It wasn't long before I discovered that much of what I believed and embraced had become contaminated with modernism in four ways:

- A Great Commission fraught with great omissions
- A misplaced confidence in human initiative, reasoning, and strategy
- Unwarranted evangelical triumphalism
- The practice of putting programs before people

A Great Commission Fraught with Great Omissions

I was taught in the early part of my Christian life that Christ established his church on earth for just one reason—to seek and win the lost in a dying world. Given this conviction, it naturally followed that success in soul winning was established as the primary criterion of Christian vitality and fruitfulness. Radical moral and social transformation was viewed either as an impossibility in a dying world or as an outcome of conversion, but not as an end in itself. To me this grossly distorted Christ's command to make disciples who would follow all that he taught and modeled.

I could not escape his call for obedience to a radical lifestyle dedicated to transforming a corrupt world through salt and light. Only later did I come to realize that Christianity had all but capitulated to the cardinal doctrine of modernism that faith, if it is to have any value at all, is confined solely to the world of personal life and values. Given this fact, it became perfectly obvious why evangelism and revival had not experienced sweeping moral, economic, and political changes—a normal and expected outcome of revival—since the 1850s.[3]

As I write these reflections, I'm stunned by the virtual silence in evangelical quarters on the widespread corruption characterizing America's business community. Why do we speak out loudly about such litmus test issues as homosexuality and abortion but remain silent about endemic public corruption? Thank God that the Two-Thirds World long ago began to break out of modernism brought by the West and has taken the lead in holistic ministry in which no distinctions are made between evangelism, personal holiness, and social transformation.

A Misplaced Confidence in Human Initiative, Reasoning, and Strategy

The evangelical movement in our lifetime has been characterized by a serious and much-needed commitment to reach the unreached worldwide through accelerated evangelism. Unfortunately evangelism increasingly became characterized by an all-out dedication to mobilizing scientific reasoning and technology to "finish the task" given by our Lord as he ascended into heaven. In so doing, too many have uncritically accepted two insidious core values of modernism:

- No task is too big and complex to defy solution.
- Bigness is a sign of greatness.

In the last half of the 20th century, a Great Commission juggernaut emerged, driven by the primary goal of numerical growth. Christians formulated and discarded strategies based on the numbers of responses. While I understood this logic and accepted it to a point, I couldn't escape from the penetrating biblical challenge "to give the reason for the hope that you have" (1 Peter 3:15). Peter assumed that others have sensed the aroma of Christ present when believers, individually and corporately, dedicate their lives to being salt and light in a lost world. In short, he was admonishing us that the words of Jesus are made flesh by the evidence of believers who are genuine salt and light. This is the message of the gospel. Words, while important, are secondary.

I contrasted this biblical perspective with prevailing practices that reduced the gospel to methods that communicated propositional truth (the plan of salvation) followed by persuasion to "receive Christ." I began to wonder: How this is different from marketing methods designed to promote consumer products? I couldn't help but conclude that we had engaged in serious biblical reductionism in which the gospel becomes little more than a consumer product marketed internationally with an abundant life message "dreams will come true" as our competitive distinctive. Our strategy called for advertising (gospel media) to generate consumer interest and personal selling (personal witness) to close the sale accompanied by public accolades for individuals and expanded donor support for organizations with the highest sales numbers.

You may have heard of the Engel scale, my attempt to convey that evangelism takes place as sensitive and caring believers relate with those seeking to discover the reasons for our hope, a process moving from the known to the unknown.[4] God calls believers to give testimony to this reality, not to persuade. In the process, Christ reveals himself and the Holy Spirit alone—not skillful human persuasion—brings about new birth. This is evangelism at its best, a fact confirmed by decades of evangelistic research, including Brian McLaren and others at the forefront of evangelism with today's postmoderns.[5]

Unwarranted Evangelical Triumphalism

Over the last 10 to 15 years I have heard many so-called experts declaring that we are on the verge of fulfilling the Great Commission based on the numbers "reached" around the world. Many looked forward to finishing the task by the beginning of a new millennium. Without doubt there is a Christian presence worldwide for the first time in history, a significant accomplishment. At the same time, immorality, corruption, and injustice within these countries have reached levels not even seen in Sodom and Gomorrah. In reality, we've only just begun when we view the totality of the Great Commission.

The bottom began to drop out of this triumphalism about a decade ago for many reasons, one of which was widespread immorality among well-known Christian leaders. The greatest shock came from Rwanda, declared by many to be our greatest missiological success on the basis that the country was 80 percent Christian and churches were bursting at the seams. Then the country was torn asunder once again by barbaric tribalism, a reality largely untouched by Christian faith. While there were many martyrs, much of the carnage was led by church people.

This underscored to me the extent to which Christianity had become little more than a veneer on society in far too many countries declared to be reached. As a professional in evaluating ministry, I saw this coming. I either led, participated in, or had access to most of the analyses of what actually took place in allegedly evangelized areas. Far too frequently the numbers proved to be little more than a mirage.

As I traveled around the world, I saw evidence of the large numbers of alleged converts who joined church ranks only to exit through the back door never to be seen again—statistics rarely made public, especially to donors. Furthermore, numbers became meaningless given the fact that so little priority was placed on discipling and unleashing new believers. Thousands of pastors worldwide have told me that fewer than 10 percent (usually 5 percent or less) are active in the faith beyond Sunday attendance.

Through the years I sounded the alarm that we were missing the mark in a serious way. Clearly we had fallen victim to a misdirected managerial missiology in which strategy took precedent over biblical principle and the lessons of the history.

The Practice of Putting Programs before People

I have often felt like an unappreciated cog in the Great Commission machinery designed to fit people into its mold with only scant attention paid to productivity, fulfillment, and well being. This mentality still prevails in many churches and organizations. Sadly it carries over from the factory era in modernism and is characterized by top-down command and conformity. It can have devastating effects on lives—even bringing people, myself included, to the point of doubting whether ministry is worth the price.

I can't remember how many times I heard the admonition that we must sacrifice everything to reach a dying world—our comforts, our personal dreams, our lives themselves. Christ made it perfectly clear that those who save their life will lose it. But does this also mean 80-hour work weeks are required and that we must put ministry ahead of everything else? I hardly think so.

What we have done is enthrone and even publicly honor evangelical workaholism, a common feature within modernism that has torn many lives and families asunder behind the scenes. I have seen little priority given to making sure that all involved in the ministry are productive and fulfilled.

Even today, I, a recent retiree, continue to be admonished that a Christian cannot step back from the firing line, turn responsibilities over to younger more capable people, and retire. I make these comments with sadness, because I am a recovering workaholic who has paid the price for my time in the evangelical spotlight.

Some Lessons Learned along the Way

In my ministry over the years, I have had the great privilege of joining hands with many others worldwide to help bring about a return to a more authentic Christianity unshackled from the contamination of modernism. Will Norton, my dean and mentor at Wheaton, and I sounded the alarm in 1975 that something had gone wrong with the harvest.[6] These issues are discussed in much greater detail in the recent book *Changing the Mind of Missions.*[7]

I'm retired now from active ministry responsibilities, but I still continue to learn as I pilgrimage with my Lord. The two foundational lessons I have learned and keep on learning are these:

- Christ came to establish and extend his kingdom.
- His primary method is spontaneous expansion of the local church.

Christ's Goal Is to Extend His Kingdom and Reign on the Earth

As I have contended above, our zeal to win the world and finish the work of Christ in our lifetime has reduced Christ's Great Commission to a great evangelistic commotion. This was indelibly impressed on me a few years back when a Christian leader from the Central African Republic spoke on behalf of many colleagues: "The missionaries brought us Christ but never taught us how to live." This summed up the truncated evangelical agenda focused mainly on evangelism to the neglect of building disciples who will transform their world.

This is tragic and demoralizing in light of Christ's goal to establish and extend his kingdom and reign on earth. Jesus announced his great mission (Luke 4:18-19) to preach the good news to the poor, to proclaim freedom for the prisoners and recovery of sight for the blind, to release the oppressed, and to proclaim the year of the Lord's favor (liberation from sin and its consequences). He called for a radically new lifestyle—the narrow way—and offered salvation to everyone willing to respond and repent.

Christ summarized his method of extending his kingdom for the disciples before his ascension. We know it as the Great Commission. He told us to make disciples, ordinary people who will do extraordinary things, by sharing the good news, baptizing those who respond, and teaching them everything that he himself taught and modeled on earth. Christ, in other words, put forth a seamless agenda with no dichotomies or variations in priority between evangelism, holy living, and social transformation.

This great truth about Christ's kingdom and reign almost completely eluded me until the first of the famous Lausanne conferences held in 1974. One leader after another from the Two-Thirds World prophetically declared that our western evangelistic preoccupation, while foundational and necessary, had not transformed the world as Christ intended.

They issued a clear call to return to a local, church-based, kingdom-focused gospel that would penetrate all of life with the lordship of Christ. Then and only then will the church have a compelling message in a pluralistic world. At their insistence, the famous but now almost forgotten and ignored Lausanne Covenant called for church-based holistic ministry that takes the entirety of the Great Commission seriously.

For many in attendance, including me, Lausanne 1 was the high-water mark of evangelical Christianity during the last century, a point of radical change in our outlook and ministry. First and foremost we heard the voice of God, confessed our failures, and changed our priorities. We began the process, continuing to this day, to break out of modernism and restore Christ's holistic balance in our response to his Great Commission. Furthermore, we celebrated the fact that momentum in the evangelical movement had shifted, once and for all, away from the west and welcomed the new wineskins that emerged.

His Method Is Spontaneous Expansion of the Local Church

Jesus left as his heritage a wonderful model to extend his kingdom and reign. He took ordinary people, often outcasts and misfits, and transformed them into extraordinary people known as disciples. Together in countercultural community—the church—they became salt and light to the lost and shook their world to its foundations. Christ made it clear that the church always would be a minority, albeit a powerful one, with a powerful transforming influence far beyond its numbers. He never said anything about having a goal for numerical growth. If growth does take place, it's an outcome of the Holy Spirit working in the lives of his people, not by grand programs and managerial expertise.

Once I was a gung-ho new believer who viewed the church as an enemy more than anything else, and I certainly wasn't alone. Many of us blamed the church for the fact that so much of our lives was spent in the pews without power or meaning, and we all but wrote the church off as a vital force. We embraced the parachurch movement as the only viable way to design strategies and mobilize the resources needed to win the world in our lifetime.

While this disdain is unfortunate, the church tends to be an institution driven by top-down professional leadership and recruitment for ever-expanding programs. The result is passive laity largely uninvolved beyond Sunday morning. Churches of this nature are an unfortunate remnant of modernism. Parachurch agencies were created to do what the church often wouldn't do beyond its walls.

I came to see that the church our Lord envisions is radically different. It exists as a community characterized by love, acceptance, and account-ability, where common people are transformed by their faith to live uncommon lives and do uncommon deeds. As a result, the work of the kingdom happens in small, often invisible ways as these common people are empowered and unleashed to be true disciples making full use of their temperaments, gifts, and outlook. Ministry programs and strategies no doubt will emerge, but they will be initiated and energized by the laity, not the leaders.

Christ knew without doubt that his disciples would always struggle to learn more about themselves and about him. His goal was to build true community characterized by love, acceptance, support, and accountability. The community itself becomes a winsome message in a divided world.

It's time to dismantle our ecclesiological machinery. A great turning point for me was when I began to realize from the history of Christian witness that the church of Jesus Christ becomes revived when it breaks out of dead orthodoxy and institutionalization and becomes an organism, not an organization. I love the vision of John Wesley that the local congregation is "a body…compacted together, in order, first, to save each his own soul; then to assist each other in working out salvation; and afterwards, as far as in them lies, to save all from present and future misery, to overturn the kingdom of Satan, and to set up the kingdom of Christ."[8]

A hero in my life is Roland Allen, a respected Anglican missionary, who shocked the missions world of an earlier day equally preoccupied with methods and strategy. He bluntly contended that the true community of believers follows the methods of the Apostle Paul and expands spontaneously through the daily life of the community, individually and corporately, under the leadership of the Holy Spirit.[9] No triumphalism here.

Spontaneous expansion is best conceptualized as a series of lights expanding in the darkness until whole areas are illuminated. Perhaps it starts with a few believers who discover one another and join together in community. This single light turns into many as believers on the narrow way demonstrate a winsome alternative to the broad way offered by the world. Most recently I've seen this process at work in war-torn parts of the Congo where whole communities have been transformed morally, economically, and politically.

Contrast this with the relatively meager, short-lasting outputs from the plethora of grand evangelistic strategies of the 20th century conceived by parachurch agencies in western countries, calling for local churches to sign on, be trained, and become involved to win the world. It is time once and for all to declare a moratorium on these well-intentioned but misguided parachurch initiatives. Fortunately enlightened leaders are now recognizing that the greatest need is to revitalize the local church to be all that the Holy Spirit intends it to be.

The Pilgrimage Continues

Thank God we have entered into a postmodern era where another generation wrestles anew with extending Christ's kingdom and reign on this earth. Contrary to some outspoken evangelical leaders of my generation, I welcome postmodernism with all of its doubts and uncertainties. I am encouraged by the fact that relationships and community are once again prized as they were prior to the insidious individualism of the past century.

Faith is being rescued from its imprisonment in the private sector of life, and the church is gradually embracing true biblical holism. Serious attention at long last is being devoted to what I call true discipleship—a process in which we come to know and understand our selves and are taught and encouraged to become responsible and productive participants in the body of Christ.

Therefore I welcome the accelerating collapse of the walls of modernism in both the Christian and secular world and applaud the courageous voices calling for sweeping change within the ranks of evangelicalism. My plea to the reformers, however, is to recognize that postmodernism, with all its virtues, is as secular as its predecessor. Don't make the mistake of so many in my generation who all but neglected the lessons to be learned from Jesus and from the history of Christian witness. We don't need another Christian infrastructure that future generations will be forced to dismantle.

How do I position myself in this interesting arena? Am I still a card-carrying evangelical? As a committed Anglican, I believe in the historic creeds of the church and in the Articles of Religion on which this faith is based. In that sense, believing Anglicans have been evangelicals long before the era of modernism when that term was introduced. I prefer to simply say I'm a believing Christian. There's no need for adjectives.

Most important, my faith is a solid rock that never moves and always provides protection, love, and assurance even though I am less certain on more peripheral doctrinal issues. While I am increasingly convicted of my own unworthiness before God, the power of his truth, love, and acceptance grows stronger. I remember when I thanked God for the first time—my birthday a few years ago—that he created me and called me as a disciple. Since then I have come to love myself in fresh ways, one of the greatest things that can happen to a struggler.

I find myself in the wonderful situation of being able to step back from the firing line. I'm blessed by having my leadership assumed by others—far more qualified than I ever could be—to address today's challenges. My role now is one of encouragement and support. My continuing prayer comes from Psalm 71:18: "Even when I am old and gray, do not forsake me, O God, till I declare your power to the next generation, your might to all who are to come."

Questions

1. Is it possible to live with the modernistic motivation to achieve success and still be involved in the "trench evangelism" that has characterized the church in the last few decades? Is this style still effective?

2. A characteristic of moderns is that many are driven to achieve success. Are postmoderns driven to achieve anything? What might that be? How does the lure of achievement get in the way of evangelism?

3. James describes effective witness as a situation in which "sensitive and caring believers relate with those seeking to discover the reasons for our hope" as Christians. Is this an ideal that can survive the rigors of the postmodern world? Why or why not?

4. How would you explain "evangelical workaholism" to another person? What do you think about James's statement that the church enthrones and publicly honors "evangelical workaholism"? Is workaholism a problem for you? For others in your life? What's the solution?

5. What will it take for the church to effectively take the holistic approach to evangelism and discipleship outlined in the Great Commission?

6. How might God intend for the church and the parachurch to coexist in the postmodern age?

CHAPTER EIGHT

Twice Liberated: A Personal Journey through Feminism
Frederica Mathewes-Green

MY FAITH AS A CHILD WAS CHRISTIAN. As an adult woman, I am Christian again. But in the middle I was something else: a feminist. Many people, of course, would say there's no contradiction, that Christians can be feminists because Jesus came for men and women equally. In a postmodern world this line of thought seems even more reasonable, since a tacit feminism is presumed by the secular world that our Christian faith seeks to reach.

What's wrong with that? Isn't salvation offered equally to women and to men? Why turn back the clock to a time of male oppression? Why deprive the world of women's gifts?

As obvious as the blueness of the sky, men and women are of equal value before God. They are equally gifted by him, and deserve equal opportunity to exercise their gifts. That's not where my uneasiness lies. It's not what feminists say, but how they say it (well, with secular feminists, sometimes it *is* what they say). An attitude of self-righteousness. A tendency to pull rank as a victim. A lack of humility. A blindness to the fact that women, just as talented as men, are just as sinful, too. Smugness, touchiness, judgmentalism, and even darker notes of condescension, ridicule, and anger toward men. Pretty much the opposite of every line in 1 Corinthians 13. My brothers and sisters, "you have not so learned Christ" (Ephesians 4:20, NKJV).

Church leaders in a postmodern age need to do some careful sifting here if they're going to accurately separate wheat from chaff. Yes, we should value and use women's gifts equally with those of men. Even though the Eastern Orthodox Church (to which I belong) doesn't ordain women, it honors as saints women who did most of the things contemporary Westerners would associate with a Protestant pastorate. Orthodox are vigilant about abiding by the witness of the faithful before us, and it's clear that from the earliest years women who were teachers, preachers, and theologians were recognized as saints. Women's ministry wasn't limited to other women; some of these saints were sought by both men and women as spiritual mothers, some went as lone evangelists to convert foreign lands, and some ruled over entire nations as empresses or queens. Historic Christianity has always recognized women's gifts—in fact, recognized them in a natural, easy-going way, without making a big deal about it. Women saints are just saints, neither more nor less than men saints. They don't get a special award for being female. Harping on their sex would strike Christians of the early centuries as obsessive and bizarre.

So my feelings about feminism are complex. It's not what you say (as long as what you're saying is that men and women stand on level ground at the foot of the Cross). It's how you say it—that superciliousness, that snide twist. That attitude is a grievous spiritual disease, and it will block the healing and transformation that is ours in Christ. It took me a long time to see this.

Feminist Beginnings

When I joined the college newspaper as a shy freshman many years ago, the editor gave me my first assignment: "Find out about all this women's lib stuff."

I was baffled as to how to do that; reports of feminism (which was then usually called *women's lib*) were just beginning to titillate the public, just beginning to show up in Johnny Carson jokes about bra burners. Was it possible to dig up any local libbers?

My editor's suggestion was to go to the Student Union and have them announce over the loudspeaker, "Anyone representing the women's liberation movement, please come to the information desk." Imagine what would happen if such a message were announced from that same desk today! But in 1970, after a slight pause, two women came steaming up, glowing with the zealot's inner flame. Kathy and Rosa steered me into the student lounge, where they opened to me the hidden knowledge of women's oppression through the ages. As they expounded this mystic wisdom, I began to nod. I liked what I was hearing.

I was ready to believe in something. I had spurned my Roman Catholic upbringing a few years before, and spent my high school years strumming antiwar songs at a hip Unitarian church. (Our elfin pastor was fond of repunctuating St. John: "God is. Love!") It was *deep*, of course, but somehow it wasn't enough, sharing superior smiles with the elbow-patch crowd and sneering at Nixon. We were pledged to reject any conviction more precise than that people are grand and everyone should be nicer to each other. I was 17, and I was looking for deeper convictions.

When my first campus byline appeared a week later, it was located over a story that cautiously endorsed the libbers. I continued my catechesis under Kathy and Rosa. The prototype-version of women's lib that they initiated me into was still searching for a focus. The movement understood itself as firmly underground and was self-consciously countercultural, even deliberately crude. Wearing suits with little bow ties and carrying briefcases was the farthest thing from our minds. We ridiculed *men* who wore suits.

The movement was a spontaneous, uncoordinated explosion of energy and anger without a clear plan and, in our case, amply fertilized by the pungent manure of ignorance. Childless, we talked about using communal baby farms to free women from the awful burden of their own children. Sexual neophytes, we talked earnestly about the Myth of the Vaginal Orgasm. As girls' dorm dwellers, we sought out the town's lesbian bar, where we were invited to dance by serious older women with arms like sides of beef. In my own body I displayed the confused zeal of the time: I stopped shaving my legs but continued plucking my eyebrows.

However, in a phase of the movement's life when it was strongly associated with the term *man-haters*, we generally got along well with men. Most of us remained enthusiastically heterosexual. We were in harmony with our brothers in the overall hippie countercultural agenda, and our enemies were not men, but straights (meaning, in those days, people who didn't smoke dope)—Young Republicans, Jesus Freaks, and the Establishment.

In my senior year a movement buddy stopped me in a hallway. She was ecstatic with the news: a woman had won a top executive job at AT&T. I was surprised at her enthusiasm. What do we want executive jobs for?

That's just a way of being co-opted, getting sucked into the establishment. The women's movement is not about trying to get a bigger piece of the pie, I insisted. We're talking about a different kind of pie altogether.

Someone scheduled a debate for an empty classroom; I represented the counterculture side. "We're selling out," I said. "We didn't start this revolution to end up with our representatives wearing tasteful jewelry and looking important on TV. Remember Joni Mitchell singing, 'You could have been more than a name on the door on the 33rd floor in the air'? Remember Harry Chapin singing about the executive father too busy to see his son, and the son saying, 'I'm gonna be like you, Dad'? Didn't we reject all that careerism and materialism as deadening to the soul? Why in the world would we want it now?"

I don't recall if I won the debate; my position certainly did not win the war. As Naomi Wolf suggests in her book *Fire with Fire*,[1] the movement came to split between Victim Feminism (self-defeating poutiness and man-blaming) and Power Feminism, which she champions. Wolf cites core principles for Power Feminism: retaliation, money and worldly power, and victory. If nothing else, it's refreshing to hear the underlying values of this philosophy described so baldly.

In Search of a Counterculture

My search for something deeper was not going to be satisfied by a women's movement that lusted after earthly power; I was truly looking for a counterculture. If I could have listened to my heart more carefully, I would have identified some of those revolutionary values as love, joy, peace, patience, kindness, and the rest of the list in Galatians 5:22-23. I searched in the New Age and age-old Eastern religions, but nothing rang true to me, and the blue gods were never more than amusing.

A month after graduation, our hitchhiking honeymoon brought my husband and me to Dublin. The late afternoon light was glaring as we stepped inside a dusty church and stood there blinking. I walked over to examine a white marble statue in the back: Jesus pointing to his Sacred Heart, which was twined with thorns and springing with flames.

I remembered the words from Sunday school: "Behold the heart that has so loved mankind." A few minutes later I realized I was on my knees. When I stood up, I was a Christian.

In the following decades as a pastor's wife—first in the Episcopal church, more recently in Holy Orthodoxy—my relationship with feminism changed even as the movement itself changed. It took me several more years to question abortion, and longer than that to question knee-jerk inclusive language demands. I attended seminary and hoped to be a priest (not a feasible goal in the mid-1970s and not my goal at all after my husband had been ordained a few years and I saw the job first hand.)

Though my husband and I still clung to the fashionable labels feminist and *liberal*, those identities were being gradually hollowed out and replaced with conservative convictions. It was hard to let our old hippie identities go. When my husband was finally compelled by conscience to vote for a Republican presidential candidate, he took along one of our young sons to actually pull the lever. He declared when he came home, "These hands are still unsullied."

I had come around to a pro-life position but didn't feel comfortable with that movement's right-wing style. When I heard of a group called Feminists for Life, I joined immediately, and when they needed a newsletter editor a few years later, I volunteered. At my first board meeting I received some surprising news: the editorship made me a vice president automatically. What's more, this was the first time the tiny organization had ever had an officer living near Washington D.C. I was deputized to get media attention for the organization. I was as perplexed about how to do this as I'd been years before when commissioned to interview women's libbers. Other members of the organization suggested that when something newsworthy happened, like a Supreme Court decision, I should go hang around and try to get on TV.

When I heard on the news on a July 1989 morning that the Supreme Court's Webster decision had been released, I put on my Feminists for Life sweatshirt—the only pro-life garment I owned—and drove into D.C. carrying stacks of a document I'd drawn up, antiabortion statements by 19th-century feminist leaders like Susan B. Anthony. Clustered all over the marble steps and landings were knots of movement leaders surrounded by knots of media people and mobile TV transmitters towered high overhead. I gave a copy of my flyer to Molly Yard who scowled at me, offended that I'd been so rude. I gave one to Bella Abzug, who lectured me that groups like mine don't really care about women. Movement leaders lined up, each waiting to give a 30-second bite for a network camera, and I tried to gather my courage to get in line. I was very hot. My husband came up to me and observed, "Your sweatshirt is working."

A couple of weeks later I got a phone call from C-SPAN, asking me to come in that evening to appear on a viewer call-in program. I knew so little about media that I thought it was a radio network and asked whether I would do the show from home. When I arrived I found that the communications director of the National Right to Life Committee was also on the show, and afterward she said she'd like to refer media calls to me in the future. A few weeks after that I was on a plane to New York, headed for ABC and a brand new show with Diane Sawyer called *PrimeTime Live*.

After that the calls kept pouring in. The media was hungry for something fresh to say about an issue that had grown stale, and Feminists for Life began drawing attention disproportionate to its meager size. Before long I'd assembled a video scrapbook of me wearing tasteful jewelry and looking important on TV. I began to get speaking invitations and to travel across the country. Events took an unexpected turn, however, when I wrote an essay to summarize the Feminists for Life position. *The Bitter Price of Choice* was widely reprinted, and soon editors were phoning me to ask for more essays; gradually, they began to ask for writing on topics other than the abortion issue. My identity as *pro-life activist* gradually changed to writer.

Calling Feminism into Question

As the years passed, the old feminist identity began to rankle me more and more. I could wear the label by applying Gloria Steinem's vague definition that it meant "the equality and full humanity of women and men." Still, I was uncomfortably aware that the average person gave the term many more connotations. Most of my Feminist for Life buddies clung to the label, insisting that it was legitimate particularly in light of the pro-life convictions of 19th-century feminist founders. But, as a writer, it worried me to use a word in ways outside the common understanding. Humpty Dumpty told Alice that he could make a word mean whatever he wanted "by paying it extra," but I didn't agree. The purpose of language is to communicate, and any living language grows according to its common use, not according to the dictates of partisan hijackers or an Academie. It seemed increasingly deceptive to have a private definition of a word different from its commonly understood meaning.

I was having trouble with the concept, not just the label. The presuppositions of feminism seemed to divide, implying that issues pertaining to women could be separated from, were more important than, other issues. My view of the human condition and the pervasiveness of sin had broadened, leading to me to the conviction that women could not ultimately win a better lot from any human agency nor could their situation be improved without helping men and children as well. We are all together in this stewpot, and we all need the same Savior; he makes no distinctions between male and female, though feminists harped on the distinctions incessantly.

Worst of all, though, was the self-pity and self-righteousness that feminism induced. I began to see in the feminist style—in fact, in the remnants of the counterculture generally—a disposition that wasn't just annoying, it was spiritually dangerous. As I looked back, I could see the roots of this attitude at the beginning in the thrilling Woodstock days when I first decided to call myself a hippie.

My husband attended the original Woodstock (he says all he remembers is "lying on the ground a lot"). I didn't go; I was too young. But in my high school bedroom I listened to the three-record set over and over and wished I had been there. Not just the music but also the announcements between the songs were fascinating, alluring. It all sounded so heroic: Joan Baez's talk about draft resistance, Arlo Guthrie's celebration of drug smuggling, references to "the pigs" that conjured an Establishment bent on oppression.

In midair above my record player, a community was forming. I wanted to be part of it. The music was great, but what really drew me was the idealism: oppose the war, resist repression, reject conformity for creativity and freedom. One morning I was driving to high school and realized it was a self-appointed state. "I can be a hippie!" At last I belonged.

I found the movement's activist style intoxicating. I thought that it was the urgency of the causes that energized me, but the causes turned out to be interchangeable. Take "mind-expanding" drugs, for instance. It seemed hip and daring to champion them, but after a year or so, nobody pretended that drugs had positive spiritual-artistic effects; we had carted too many of our friends to the emergency room. Drug use continued, but it was impossible to continue to treat it as a cause. So we stopped making absurd claims for psychedelia, and found other things to make claims about, our hip-and-daring stance intact. The cause didn't matter, the attitude did; attitude was more addictive than pot.

Free love was another temporary cause. Early hippies proposed that, in some vague, groovy way, the incidence of lovemaking in the world actually created love in the world, and if there was enough of it, the Tantric waves would end the war in Vietnam. Girls wanted to believe this, wanted to be as carefree as men, but too often were shocked to find themselves feeling heartbroken and abandoned. Free sex continued, but we stopped pretending it was a cause.

Other causes were handy enough though. I put pro-abortion buttons on my smock at work, and intimidated customers at the campus lunch counter out of eating their nonunion lettuce.

It wasn't the causes that energized us, it was the delicious feeling of being a person with a cause. This crusading persona was the perfect solution to adolescent confusion and angst. Suddenly I felt like a hero, strong and wise and true. I was liberated to be the absolutely wonderful person I truly was.

That's what I thought, anyway. In truth, I was turning into a self-righteous, self-dramatizing prig. I could have easily done this on my own, but the seeds of attitude lofted about in the wake of Woodstock found fertile soil in my teenage psyche.

The causes came and went. When they went, what was left behind was good old narcissism, the most durable fuel known to humankind. What remained was attitude, a delicious self-admiring gaze, wondering at the expansiveness of our own valor. It's astonishing how this little germ of attitude grew and spread. Joan Baez describes a prison hunger strike with only the faintest edge of smugness in her voice; 30 years later everyone is a self-made hero. Bigwigs and entertainment royalty pull a long face and appear on TV talk shows to deplore some pipsqueak bigot, even an imaginary one. We peons join in by buying goods with *Save the Earth!* stamped on the package. We savor the idea that we're marching boldly against some foe—a Lex Luthor-type who lives under Manhattan and is pro-pollution, perhaps.

It's All about the Superman Cape

I imagine a small boy with a pillowcase pinned to his shoulders like a Superman cape, standing on his bed so he can see himself in the bureau mirror. The Superman cape is our culture's most common fashion statement. Feminism is only one of its many expressions; the causes, as I said, are interchangeable. It's an intoxicating costume. For one thing, the Superman cape works like an invisibility cloak in reverse: put it on and you can't see your own faults. Instead, you see everyone else's with lightning clarity and presume the authority to judge them.

What's more, Superman-Cape Attitude has no natural enemies. If opposition arises—and self-made heroes secretly hope it will—it just proves that the hero threatens the powers-that-be. An episode of opposition gives you a delicious opportunity to display your valor. Self-criticism or awareness of one's own flaws is impossible because external criticism reinforces the conviction that you're right.

There's a logical problem in the uniformity of self-appointed heroism. How can we be standing valiantly against the crowd, when the crowd is packed in around us tight as sardines? But this attitude is not much troubled by logic. We bravely support all those unpopular causes championed by the most powerful institutions of media, entertainment, and academia. Being a brave defender of unpopular causes is a whole lot easier, now that most recognizable causes are fabulously popular. Furrowed brow, steely gaze, all that, in the docile safety of conformity.

Spiritually, the Superman cape brings great danger. It blinds us to our own faults, so exhilarated are we by the faults of others. We develop contempt for others and describe them and their beliefs in the language of insult. We can become addicted to anger, an explosive and thrilling emotion. I have heard speakers actually urge their audiences to stay angry, as if this were a constructive state. The saying is true: anger is an acid that destroys its container. It leads us to see our opponents as subhuman, as not deserving of rights. It leads us to see ourselves as perfect, heroic, immortal. Fortunately we are not immortal. We are on a planet together hurtling through space, and we have only this lifetime to love one another.

The Superman costume is like the shirt of Nessus, a wedding gift to Hercules that was supposedly charged with supernatural power. In reality, it was saturated with poison. He could not peel it off as it burned away his skin. I began to see that feminism was bad for me. It inculcated feelings of self-righteousness and judgmentalism. It filled me with self-perpetuating anger. It blinded me to the good that men do and the bad that women do. It made me think that men and women were enemies, when we actually have a mutual Enemy—who delights in any human discord.

I even began to think that the whole theory was erroneous—that men and women rise and fall together, their situation affected by race or class, but not gender. A housemaid has more in common with her short-order cook husband and her bricklayer brother than with the wealthy female lawyer whose toilet she cleans. Of all the ways that genuine injustice can appear, gender seemed increasingly the most spurious grid to use. I began to suspect the whole thing was a sham. It was that we wanted to be victims too. Victims have power. Feminism allowed half the human race to claim instant victim status, no matter how much material comfort we enjoyed. It was irresistible, and, I was starting to think, it was a lie.

After a few years of representing Feminists for Life, I was having increasing doubts about the first part of that label. When *Christianity Today* asked me for an essay presenting pro-life feminism I complied but wondered if I was doing the right thing. When the editor requested changes making the feminist angle more prominent, I felt the screws tightening. I rewrote the piece, and as soon as I'd submitted it I phoned the Feminists for Life office and said I was ready to retire. I could no longer call myself a feminist. The journey that had begun that day in the student lounge, as Kathy and Rosa eagerly expounded the faith, had come to an end.

I still hold some convictions I gained during my feminist journey—ideas about the goodness of our natural bodies, about the intrinsic equal value of men and women, about the right every person should have to prove their abilities without prejudice. But even now, as I travel and speak around the country, I continue to meet Christian women who have adopted the feminist self-righteous, self-flattering tone.

I don't know how to tell them this, because that Superman cape repels every dart, but I wish I could: the only path to salvation, to transformation in Christ, is by humility and repentance. Pray for the grace to see your own sins; pray that you may not fall into the trap of judging others. Consider yourself the chief of sinners, not the chief of the sinned-against. Stop scrutinizing your experience, looking for examples of offenses; love keeps no account of wrongs.

Turn it around. Serve others. Forgive. Feminism isn't liberation. It's a complicated trap. True freedom comes from someplace—Someone—else.

Questions

1. How do social issues distract us from the true purpose of the gospel? Engage us in the true purpose of the gospel?

2. Why do many people become engaged with advancing a social cause but lack zeal for advancing the gospel?

3. Do we as ministers of the gospel face the same temptation to become

"self-righteous, self-dramatizing prigs" that Frederica faced in her feminist crusade? What can we do to prevent this from happening?

4. The Superman cape that Frederica speaks of acts as an "invisibility cloak in reverse; put it on and you can't see your own faults. Instead, you see everyone else's with lighting clarity and presume the authority to judge them." How has the Superman cape affected the church? Affected you?

5. For those who wear the Superman cape, "self-criticism or awareness of one's own flaws is impossible because external criticism reinforces the conviction that you're right." Have you found yourself wearing the Superman cape? How can you move in step with postmodernism but avoid this problem?

CHAPTER NINE

Worldview Therapy
Earl Creps

I AM A CLASSICAL PENTECOSTAL WHO LIVES IN TWO WORLDS. One is the American version of my movement that is clinging to cultural terrain rapidly being submerged by something unfamiliar. Both our homespun rural origins and our newfound suburban respectability feel increasingly isolated from the post-Christian world that I study and live in. Too often my movement has reacted by becoming strident and defensive. Both are signs that this crisis is real.

The modernist culture I was prepared to reach is being immersed in postmodernism—the world I now live in. Postmodernism obviously wasn't covered in my correspondence school ministry training. I am often reminded of the scene in the otherwise forgettable *Waterworld* in which Kevin Costner and Jeanne Tripplehorn tour the underwater ruins of a preapocalyptic civilization. They find everything from city streets to apartment buildings and a sunken submarine.[1]

The modern world is also still down there, but it's becoming more of a memory and less of an influence. If you can forgive my pressing the metaphor one more notch, like Costner, my goal is *dry land*. I have no desire to live submerged in the past, but neither am I content to drift aimlessly on the surface of cultural trends. Identity is the critical issue. What am I now? And what must Pentecostalism look like to make a positive contribution in the new world?

Rewind

Let's put the issues into rewind for a moment.

As a child, I experienced the rural Pentecost of my mother's Maryland hometown during family vacations. I can still see red-faced preachers, blue veins throbbing in their temples, thundering the faith to the faithful—quite a contrast for a Lutheran pastor's son being raised in the cool reserve of an urban, liturgical church.

The former group had lively music and claimed to possess all the answers. People did strange things during their services—really strange. The latter group had gothic music and did not seem interested in the questions. Their services were marked by solemnity. My Pentecostal relatives measured the truth of a thing by how *loudly* it was said, while my liturgical elders knew a thing was true by how *often* it was said (from the service book). One communion measured validity by *volume*, the other by frequency. Every group has some standard for this sort of thing. I suppose the only question is which standard they use.

Having been buffeted by both extremes, I washed up on the shores of late adolescence convinced that I could walk a path right down the middle, guided by a general skepticism, to create a Switzerland-like state of spiritual neutrality. To my young eyes, the Pentecostal strain in the family seemed to carry emotionalism, ignorance, and an amazing ability to use the same tongue for both glossolalia and vicious gossip. Meanwhile, our liturgical wing involved too much dead tradition, too many church dinners, and the bleak irrelevance of the religion we were practicing to the life we lived. In the final analysis I wanted to avoid both ends of my spiritual gene pool.

Only much later did I understand the premodern perspective assumed by my Pentecostal relations, and the very different modern foundations of my more upscale mainline home congregation. This culture gap would prove prophetic of the two worlds in which I currently hold dual citizenship.

Testing Positive for Glossolalia

My carefully planned spiritual neutrality collapsed under the impact of the Charismatic Renewal in my denomination. I watched liturgical folk become charismatics in quantity while classical Pentecostals looked on in disbelief. Surely, Teutonic, beer-sipping Lutherans were not eligible for the fullness of the Spirit! Surely BMW-driving Episcopals would never be permitted to speak in tongues! Other Pentecostals were smug: at last our poor mainline cousins had caught up with the chosen people.

Despite both the natural resistance of a Germanic church culture and the arrogance of Pentecostal commentators, I came to faith in a revelatory moment during a Lutheran service and was filled with the Spirit in a skeptical Methodist pastor's living room a few weeks later. All of this would take place as I was preparing to leave home for college. I entered adulthood as a card-carrying, on-fire, Spirit-filled, hippy, charismatic, Lutheran Jesus freak.

P.C.

Then something happened. After lots and lots of secular education, I felt a call to vocational ministry while in my first university teaching job. Ironically I found a position as a volunteer staff member in an Assemblies of God church, the denomination of my Pentecostal aunts and uncles. Somehow, they didn't seem so alien now.

I became an apprentice. The senior pastor was a mentor to me, the church was wonderful, and the professional growth was outstanding. But something else was happening, something that I never saw coming. The hippy Jesus freak of my youth was cooling off into a right-from-the-factory, shrink-wrapped Assemblies of God minister. I was becoming P.C.—Pentecostally Correct.

But this was a new Pentecost, very unlike what I saw as a child in the coalfields of Maryland. We were suburban, respectable, and upwardly mobile. Our support staff had computers. Our people got promotions at work. Our church was big for the area. Our programming grew weekly. Our building expanded. Our pastors used hair gel. By God, we were just as good as the Baptists! In our hearts, we had moved to the 'burbs, thinking that the virtues of our small town premodernism would migrate with us.

We were wrong.

Suburbia was having the same effect on us that it had on everything else it touched. We were being domesticated, tamed so we would fit in with the predictability and comfort that suburbanites have come to see as one of their inalienable rights.[2] We were also being gradually assimilated into the broader modernist evangelical subculture with its tendency to regard the supernatural as absolute in Bible history, but suspect in the present.[3]

The bland were leading the bland. We had stopped being dangerous a long time ago. We saw some fruit, but in the end, instead of going to the nations, we were bound for Wal-Mart. I would become an unwitting carrier for the P.C. virus in my next two churches. Willing hosts awaited me wherever I went.

Slowly, both the premodern simplicity of what Peter Wagner would call my First Wave relatives and the experiential openness of my Second Wave charismatic peers were morphing into something else.[4] My Pentecostal identity and my professional ministry were being dissolved into baby boomer modernism like sugar into espresso. You can taste the sweetness, but there's no doubt that it's still espresso.

The farther I went in ministry, the more Christianity became a set of ideas and the ministry a kind of technology I used. I preached many services that were "Pentecostal" only because someone had the nerve to launch an utterance in tongues during the pause between the slow songs and the announcements. It was the worst of both worlds. I had just enough modern skepticism to be jaded about the supernatural, but not enough scientific leadership technique to implement a successful substitute.

Deconstruction of a Pentecostal

The purgatory of semimodernism into which I had stumbled was a depressing place to live. My first church, almost all boomers, had grown some (before the split), but not enough to get any notices in the denominational district newsletter. My second church, mostly builders, wanted to attract younger people while remaining traditional enough to keep the older saints happy. They had invented a whole new kind of purgatory. When our two forms of misery met, my theological heritage and ministry techniques were exposed as both contradictory and ineffective.

Was it me?

Was it God?

Was it them?

I was deconstructed.

Two things saved me. The first was the controversial season of revival that Pentecostals and others began to experience in the mid 1990s. Ironically, a First Wave emphasis on repentance and a Third Wave focus on love somehow found me in the ruins of my modernized Second Wave spirituality. Repentance revealed my almost complete self-involvement. It hurt. Love helped me believe that I might actually have some role in the kingdom of God after all. I needed both. Together these forces moved my spiritual center of gravity away from modernity and back toward experiencing a relationship with God.

The second force was brought to bear by other Christians. The third church we served was mostly busters. Despite my age, somehow I fit best with this group. They seemed to have a natural immunity to the P.C. virus and an innate suspicion of the idea that ministry was a subset of scientific management. Thinking I could influence them, they actually began to influence me.

The most noticed change in my self-righteous midwestern city was that I stopped wearing suits on Sunday. But that was a small thing. Much bigger was that my parishioners were asking different questions from the ones I was prepared to answer. This became apparent in staff meetings when I watched my mostly Gen-X team members go into suspended animation during my boomer-style training talks. As soon as I finished, they revived. The glaze on their eyes was more than boredom; it was a desire to get on with things that mattered, kingdom things like mission, compassion, authenticity, and community, rather than listening to speeches about what we might do. At first I told myself this was just another generational trait.

On Being Antediluvian

It's probably true that post-boomer age groups tend to have the traits of my young congregation in much greater intensity than their elders. Ultimately, however, I sensed that something larger was going on here, something that could not be explained simply by a person's year of birth. This was big casino, with more on the line than which church model best suits which demographic. These kids didn't just have different values; they actually lived in a different world than I did. One planet—two worldviews. Think of it.

I began searching for ways to interpret what was happening and to explore what it would mean to build an apostolic community among young adults. This search led me to *The Church on the Other Side*[5] and to other Pentecostals who were reading similar books. To my surprise I discovered a growing underground movement of young Pentecostal leaders who were investigating these issues out of their vexation with the irrelevance of the church—even Pentecostal church. What did we need to change: methods, doctrines, styles, haircuts? For many of them, it was all on the table, including Pentecostalism itself. Had we outgrown our usefulness in post-Christian America?

Lubricated by countless cups of coffee, my mind opened to the possibility that I was feeling the G forces of making the postmodern turn: the individualistic, rational, scientific skepticism of modernity was being supplanted by the communal, experiential, constructivist spirituality of postmodernity. The words of one Hollywood pretty boy summarize the hardedge postmodern life: "I don't believe in truth. I believe in style." Of course the most radical views are probably dwarfed by a more common soft or conservative postmodernity, which tends to be more about eclectic style and relativism than about continental philosophy and epistemology.

The desire for a map of the postmodern turn led to a lot more reading and to an ongoing series of field visits and interviews around the country with leaders who were connecting with emerging culture. As I documented their experiences, I clarified my own. The tide of an unfamiliar worldview was rising around me. I had three choices: drown, build higher levees, or learn to swim. Younger leaders raised in this social space grew up swimming so what was alien to me was quite natural for them. When I asked a Californian pastor, for example, whether he ever taught his young congregation about postmodernism, he replied bluntly, "That would be like telling fish about water."

This wasn't going to be pretty. The boomer in me had assumed that my cohort was destined to represent the cultural edge or at least the first-class cabin of the mainstream. Getting to know younger emerging leaders made the truth plain: I am an *antediluvian* raised before the flood, whose best hope is swimming lessons administered by those more comfortable with the water.[6] Simultaneously, I can't forget that much of the church and many of my friends live either below the surface or on patches of culture that soon will be. Since all of the church belongs to Jesus, and since both levels will be around for my lifetime, I had to begin working on being a hybrid, a guy with the ability to swim and to dive, in an effort to communicate in love with both groups.[7]

The thing about knowledge is that once you have it, you can never go back to what you were. So now, whether swimming or diving, I have to figure out what it means to be Pentecostal in a postmodern climate and to ask whether that's the same as being a postmodern Pentecostal. It's still all about identity. Who am I? Who are we? What if there were support groups for those afflicted by these issues?

M. A.

Wednesday, 7:00 p.m., a small city in the Midwest

"My name is Earl. And...and...I'm a modernist." There. I had finally said it publicly.

"Hey, everybody, let's give it up for Earl!" enthused the man with the small red flower tattoo on his forearm.

Moderate applause.

"We're really glad you could make it tonight. It's all about being real, man. I'm Dave, and I'm just like you. We all are!"

"But how did I come to this?" I wondered inside my head. "How can I be in recovery for what seemed so reasonable just a few months ago?" My vexation must have shown.

"We know how hard this is for you, bro." Dave's tone was so empathetic, so merciful. He really *did* understand this from the inside. The other group members nodded their endorsement. They were tribal looking, but strangely benevolent, not nearly as fierce as some of their body piercings.

The acceptance in the air was like a vacuum drawing the words out of me: "I just don't get it. Until a year ago I had never even *heard* of modernism. I was doing just fine, leading my ministry, preaching my sermons, planning my programs, and then the wheels fall off! A conference, a couple books, a few Web sites later, and I'm all messed up."

"Hmmm…been there…been there," they murmured among themselves.

"Well," interjected Dave, "the first step is to admit that you have a problem and that you're powerless to do anything about it."

"I'm sick of admitting my problems," I shot back. "The last year has been nothing but problems. I start out thinking that being the answer man—the expert—is what ministry is all about. Then I start wondering if that's really Christianity or just modernism or what? Great. Just great."

"Easy man, easy," soothed Dave. "At least you *know* your worldview is diseased. Most guys are still in denial about the whole deal. It took me years to face the truth."

"That's right," said a voice from the back of the room. "I just started coming a couple weeks ago. Before that I was still pretending the world was this nice orderly, rational place like some public library or something."

Several shook their heads knowingly.

"It carried over into my faith, big time. And I even inflicted it on people in sermons. I can't believe the monster I was. And I didn't even know it. At least you *know*."

Perplexed, I needed answers—right now. "So what do I actually *do* about this? How do I get free of this thing?"

"Well, that's just it," a level voice replied from the second row. "You're never actually free of the disease; it's what you are, man. But you *can* stay in recovery. We've all had to be postmodern one day at a time—right?"

Another murmur of unanimity.

"So what's the plan? What do I do?" I pleaded softly.

"Well, you start by reading the *Big Book of Postmodernism*," replied Dave. Then you just keep telling the truth and coming to M.A. meetings. Together, we can all make it."

More murmurs.

"Thank God for Modernists Anonymous."

Worldview Therapy

Having pastored three generations in three churches I now work for my denomination's only seminary. A major part of my responsibility is research and teaching on emerging culture and emerging church issues. My struggle has become my specialty, so I have decided the best way to help myself is to help others who are also riding out the cultural turn. The G forces are high enough to be painful for everyone. At a recent ministers meeting, for example, I administered a survey to the house asking three questions. Here are the answers supplied on an index card by one presumably young Pentecostal minister:

1. Is the ministry harder than it used to be? *Yes.*

2. What are your two to three biggest leadership challenges? *Leadership is too traditional, change (the lack of), too much old school (not reaching the postmoderns).*

3. What one word best describes your life right now? *Confused about the A/G. "Considering leaving."*

Today, I am connecting with those who harbor these doubts about mainstream Pentecost all over the country and with those who harbor doubts about the doubters. The former are the swimmers, the latter are the divers. Strangely, my charismatic Lutheran starting point and my role at our seminary, give me a "neutral" vantage point from which I can engage both moderns and postmoderns within the movement.

I call this experience *worldview therapy*. You might say I do anger management for Pentecostal leaders under 35 and grief recovery for those over 35. As a self-taught worldview therapist, I try to work with these different groups out of my own struggle, rather than from a posture of expertise, because there are no experts. My conviction is that in a diverse fellowship everyone should have a seat at the table. Condemning each other over issues of paradigms and piercings is not an option if we plan to survive.

When doing worldview therapy—WT—I may use a variety of methods. WT can be administered 1-to-1 with individual leaders or in a group therapy mode using a hotel conference room full of boomer AG pastors. Medication is also frequently prescribed in the form of caffeine. Exceptional coffee is the Prozac of WT.

But the key is to work diverse clients through the same issues. When the session is over, the commonality of their struggle is the adhesive that can hold them together. Here are some points I often make during our sessions. Some are hard questions; others are confrontational statements. Almost all of them I owe to someone else, because WT is, at its heart, a collaborative affair.

- *When I subtract modernity, what percentage of my Christianity is left?* (Thanks to Todd Hunter, www.postmodernmission.org.)

- *When I subtract culture, what percentage of my Pentecostalism is left?* (Thanks to my first Masters class at Northwest College.)

- *Modernism is not a disease; postmodernism is not the cure.* Postmodernism is more of a Rorschach test, saying as much about the observer as the thing observed. Given the huge pressure many of us live under to be culture-current, it pays to keep your head. Two years from now, no one may be talking about postmodernism.

- *Multiple cultural layers currently occupy the same social space.* Talking of premodernity or modernity in the past tense is simply naïve. Postmodernism is growing in influence, but it's only one of several worldviews with large followings. It's all out there, and no one knows what's next. (Thanks to Craig Van Gelder.)

- *Pentecost and postmodernism have many natural points of contact.* Experiential spirituality and the emphasis on the supernatural are only two of the possible bridges. (Thanks to Len Sweet and Brian McLaren.)

- *Postmodernism is essentially a folk religion.* The average postmodern knows nothing of French literary criticism and can't even spell *Foucault.* He or she is practicing an eclectic, almost superstitious spirituality that squares nicely with the definitions of *folk religion* that missiologists have been using for many years. Thinking of postmodernism this way makes everything simpler and less frightening.

- *Missiology is the big dog.* Don't worry too much about continental philosophy. Worry more about exegeting popular culture and reading missiology as applying to post-Christian America. (Thanks to Assemblies of God Theological Seminary President Byron Klaus and to Brad Sargent.)

- *Everything you believe about postmoderns is true*—somewhere. Neither Postmodernism (the philosophy) nor postmodernity (the culture) is just one thing. For every tattooed martini club rocker there is a spiritualist mainstreamer in khakis. It's more accurate to think of postmodernism*s*—plural. (Thanks to Millard Erickson.)

- *Pentecostals can be missional among postmoderns without fear.* Loving postmoderns is no more dangerous to our faith than loving anyone else. In fact we can learn a lot from their critique of the church and their celebration of diversity, among other attributes. All of this can be appreciated for what it is without compromise.

- *One-size-fits-all Pentecostalism is no longer viable.* The hyperdiverse future of culture will require a hyperdiverse church. No more off-the-rack solutions. Innovation is going to happen, the only question is whether it will happen in Pentecostal ranks or be exiled to more receptive territory.

- *Pentecostals need to rediscover their spiritual DNA.* We need to be more Pentecostal, not less. But we'd better figure out what that means, separating style from substance. How did we get this far in the first place? (Thanks to my favorite aunt, Mabel, a Pentecostal evangelist from the 1930s until her last breath.)

- *Pentecostals have to make the mission of the church the priority.* When we aren't doing something dangerous and missional, we get stupid in a hurry. The Spirit flows to mission, not to style or doctrine. (Thanks to Darrell Guder in *The Continuing Conversion of the Church.*)

- *Pentecostals have to find a third way between histrionic primitivism and jaded pragmatism.* We can be both powerful and credible, but only if we learn how to merge our spirituality with our strategy, instead of developing clever ways to let one substitute for the other. (Thanks to Grant Wacker in *Heaven Below*.)

- Blessing should cascade down from the older generations to the younger. Innovators should enjoy a paternal blessing from the builder generation and a fraternal blessing from the boomers. My generation needs to hold the door open for younger leaders and help finance their initiatives. (Thanks to emerging Pentecostal leaders Mark Miller and Kevin Salkil.)

- Fundamentalism is not an option. Angry defensiveness proves that everything postmoderns think about us is correct.

- This really is happening. We can deny it—but only by being intellectually Amish. (Thanks to Brian McLaren.)

When working through these therapeutic issues, healing is not defined as deprogramming postmoderns or as converting moderns into postmoderns. Boomers look silly in buzz cuts. Healing is for all of us to become better Christians.

Barbarians at the Gates

Pentecostals are not evangelicals who speak in tongues. When our hearts are soft, our experience is about a kind of Spirit fullness that overflows into our worldview, shifting it from Christian naturalism toward Christian supernaturalism, and shifting us from maintenance to mission. Pentecostals are all about getting full of God so we can announce that his kingdom is the only real world and that it's arriving among us. This trumps the Enlightenment. The arrival of this kingdom in power and the challenge of making that announcement always change us during the journey.

The reverse, however, is also true. When our hearts are hardened by arrogance or fear, we shift back into a defensive posture that concentrates on conserving what we have—which is considerable at this point in our history. The barbarians seem to be massing just outside the gates, and we rush to erect the bulwarks that will keep them outside our holy city. I see the choice between these two postures (mission versus defense) as the core decision Pentecostals have to make in the next few years. In light of what we claim to be, the choice is simple: open the gates.

My plan for the future is to simultaneously sort through the DNA of Pentecost looking for the real deal, document effective leadership strategy in the emerging church, and probe culture to find our connections to it—hopefully mapping a third way. This pursuit gives me a greater love for the whole church. Traditional or emerging, it's all Christ's body. No part of that body is served well by surrendering to utter relativism or by retreating into a fortress of neofundamentalism. Neither modernity nor Azusa Street is the pivot of history—the cross is. So I will continue to practice worldview therapy while searching for my own answers, trusting that on the journey we will all find our way to the cross.

Questions

1. Are you caught between the roots of your faith and the emerging culture of tomorrow's church? How are you adapting?

2. Earl describes the influence of suburbia on his church. It became domesticated and tamed. "The bland were leading the bland." Does that always happen? How can the influence be reversed when necessary?

3. Look back at the list of questions and statements Earl uses as part of his Worldview Therapy on page 157-159. Which do you most strongly affirm? Which are new thoughts for you? Which are most alarming?

4. What aspects of premodernist and modernist histories are beneficial for the church to integrate with postmodernity as it emerges?

5. Have you seen yourself as a modern wanting to deprogram postmoderns? As a postmodern wanting to convert moderns?

6. Earl writes, "Healing is for all of us to become better Christians." What can you do to promote healing?

STORIES OF FAITH CRISIS

CHAPTER TEN

"I Told You We Weren't Crazy!"
Brad Cecil

I WAS A FIRST-YEAR SEMINARY STUDENT IN 1991 WHEN IT HIT ME. During my Biblical Intro class, another seminary student asked the professor what seemed to be a harmless question: "Could you interpret this passage to mean _____?" It was an honest question with a valid consideration of the text, but I will never forget the professor's response: *"You could, but you would be wrong."*

I sat stunned for a minute and thought:
"You could, but you would be wrong"?

No discussion, no clarification, no consideration for the student's vantage point, no dialogue over possibilities. Just *"You could, but you would be wrong."*

The professor honestly believed he was right and therefore all other options could only be wrong. His response hit me like a load of bricks falling from the top of a 30-foot scaffold. At this point in my journey, it wasn't beyond me to give a similar response to a question like that. I was confident that my beliefs were right and all other options could only be wrong. But hearing someone else proclaim this kind of certainty seemed so odd to me. I couldn't figure out why exactly—after all, I was trained to be certain. I built my belief with a foundational epistemology. I understood the laws of noncontradiction. I believed there is only one correct interpretation of the text, meaning there could be only one right interpretation but many wrong interpretations. I felt rational. Et cetera, et cetera, et cetera.

The professor's response just didn't ring true with me. I thought to myself: *Was it his attitude? Was it his tone? Was it the environment of the seminary classroom? What was it exactly that wasn't sitting well with me?* I realized it was none of these circumstantial issues. Something much deeper was bugging me.

As I thought through this event and my new dilemma, I slowly began to understand how the professor could make this proclamation of certainty. It was based on a foundation of assumptions he trusted and didn't question. The professor held these as first-order assumptions—objective, universal, absolute. I realized he was right only if you first agreed to his assumptions about language. He was right *only* if you first agreed to his conceptual understandings . He was right *only* if you first agreed to his hermeneutic position. He was right *only* if you first agreed to his particular dispensational grid. He was right *only* if you first agreed to his many assumptions.

I thought through this theological transaction, and I started to consider all the religious positions that exist, the many assumptions this represents and how they all claim rightness with certainty on any particular scriptural interpretation. I realized the failure of "certainty" and also how much is presumed upon God, the Bible, and the world. It saddened me to consider how limited we are by our many assumptions and how marginalizing we have become with our theologies.

The professor was my inspiration to search for another way to understand God and theology (even though he didn't mean to). I took my first steps in my journey into the postmodern milieu.

At this point, I was an evangelical of the fundamentalist persuasion. In college I came to embrace evidentiary apologetics, fundamentalism, literalism, dispensationalism, conservative theology, and evangelical eschatology. After college I went to work for an evangelical youth organization as a youth camp director and youth speaker. I spoke to thousands of kids at camp in the summer and traveled the country speaking to even more youth and young adults about the certainty of the Scriptures, Christian beliefs, and God. I boldly proclaimed my view of Scripture as right and all other positions as wrong and surrounded myself with people who believed like me.

So my quandary was especially hard on me. In fact, I thought I might be losing my faith—or worse, becoming a liberal. I had heard of this happening with students in secular schools, but I didn't expect this result from attending seminary. I finally heard what I sounded like—as if I had played a recording—and I did *not* like what I heard! What seemed odd was that I didn't feel like I was turning from God; my desire for God was growing. I was hungry for God.

My family and I moved to Dallas-Fort Worth in 1991 so I could attend seminary. I had been in full-time ministry for eight years, but I wanted additional Bible knowledge for my personal struggles and to be adequately prepared for further ministry. At that time I felt God leading us to the mission field to work with the marginalized and the poor of the world.

It was a big step for us, a step of faith. I had some money in the bank but no job lined up and no ministry lined up. We were leaving our friends and family. When we arrived in Dallas-Fort Worth, we felt alone but confident that we were where God wanted us.

After settling into our new home in Arlington, Texas, my first priority was to find a job. I loved working with youth and young adults, so I sought work that would allow me to pursue this passion. I took a position at a shelter for homeless teenagers. The shelter took in more than 300 homeless youth a year and served thousands of youth and families in crisis intervention through many community service programs. The youth came to us off the streets and from some of the most horrific situations imaginable. We provided emergency shelter and tried to reunite them with their families.

Even though I loved working in the shelter where I saw God work in incredible ways, I came with the same priority as many evangelicals when it comes to social service: The world is a sinking ship, and our highest priority is to get people into lifeboats—to get them saved. All social action was just rearranging deck chairs or playing music while the ship goes down. I used to say, "It makes no sense to have someone warm or well fed if they end up in hell for eternity." In my mind social action- and compassion-based service were only valid if someone had the opportunity to share the gospel in the process of delivery.

At first I considered my job at the shelter as secular and the seminary as sacred, but my experience proved otherwise. God was at work at the shelter, which became a special place to me. I loved the staff members and their tireless dedication to youth. I loved helping the kids who were in such desperate need. I loved giving "a cup of cold water." God was drawing me close and showing himself to me through the needy youth we served. Though the work was by far the most demanding and difficult I have ever done, it was one of the most amazing times in my life.

My seminary experience was juxtaposed with my shelter experience, and in many ways I was learning more about the work of God at the shelter than at the seminary.

We started attending Pantego Bible Church in Arlington. The church was in transition with a new pastor and a new seeker-friendly approach. We plugged in and started building relationships within the church community. In 1993 the student ministry pastor position opened up. The senior pastor, Randy Frazee, knowing my background in youth work, asked me to help lead the student ministry program in the transition and to consider the position or be on the search committee for a suitable candidate. I agreed to help during the transition and with the search.

God led us to one of my friends: Joe Centineo. I agreed to work with Joe for a year until the transition was complete. With Joe joining the team, the church, which had already been growing, took off. It was exciting. The whole community was buzzing about the church. I was glad to be a part of it, but I was still disquieted within my soul. Even with the growth and the excitement, I felt something was missing.

I was doing everything a good Christian should be doing. Even my job was compassion-based service, but something was wrong. Maybe I was slipping into liberalism. Maybe I was just going through a phase. Maybe the experience during my first year at seminary had germinated and was growing...

That first-year experience motivated me to deconstruct my theology, to seek philosophical alternatives, to find new ways of building belief without certitude. I stumbled onto *The Web of Belief* by W. V. Quine.[1]

Quine introduced me to the concept of foundationalism and demonstrated how Descartes' Enlightenment ideal failed to find an irreducible starting place to build all knowledge upon. In this little book Quine discusses how difficult it is to find a universally accessible foundation to build everything else upon. He pointed out how concepts are culturally shaped and shared. Quine suggests that we don't build on a foundation at all, but rather we build *into* a web. We build our knowledge on a collection of relationships, concepts, experiences, and beliefs—all of which are continually adjusted to accommodate dilemmas, experiences, observations, and new understandings.

My first step down the road of deconstruction was to recognize that postfoundationism might be a better approach to faith.

My second step was to recognize the concept of *contingency*. I came across *Philosophical Investigations* by Ludwig Wittgenstein,[2] who pointed out what a poor job language does to convey reality: *"Why can't I describe the aroma of coffee?"* Wittgenstein suggests that language works, but claiming absolutes is difficult because of language's inherent limitations.

At first Wittgenstein's proposal didn't sit well with me, because I realized the priority we place on language, especially in the Christian community. Gradually I observed language games that we play, and I realized the need for a new conceptual understanding of language.

I came across Jacques Derrida, David Tracy, Stanley Fish, Richard Rorty, and others. I was exposed to the term *postmodernism*. I was scared initially since I hadn't heard the term in Christian circles. I thought it must be another secular attempt to destroy the foundation of the Christian faith. Still, some of the thought leaders' ideas made sense to me. I felt somewhat better after reading *Evangelicalism and the Future of Christianity* by Alister McGrath.[3] He calmed my fears about postmodernism but fueled my desire for a new expression of faith.

> The rise of the movement that is generally known as postmodernism is a direct result of both the collapse of this confidence in reason and a more general disillusionment with the so-called modern world…There has been a widespread collapse of confidence in the Enlightenment trust in the power of reason to provide foundations for a universally valid knowledge of the world, including God…It is important in this context to appreciate that it is young people, especially those engaged in academic studies, who are most acutely aware of the death of the Enlightenment and the rise of postmodernism. This has merely reinforced the attraction of

evangelicalism to this age group and highlighted how out of touch some of the leaders of the mainline denominations seem to be.

I felt McGrath was right. Many Christian leaders are out of touch, and postmodernism may provide a better playing field for Christianity. I was especially intrigued by the discussions on religion that were occurring by "secular" postmodern thought leaders. It became apparent faith was back, especially on the college campus—a place I always thought to be a bastion of secularism. I also noticed the tools being developed by postmodern thought leaders are better than the enlightenment tools to work with in developing ministry.[4] I stayed quiet and "pondered all these things in my heart."

> *There can be little doubt that we are in a wholly new interpretive situation. While this new pluralistic, postmodern situation is perceived by many as a threat to "mainline" churches and to the long-settled claims of conventional text reading, it is my judgment, and my urging that the new situation is in fact a positive opportunity to which interpreters of the Bible may attend with considerable eagerness.[5]*

In 1995 I was still volunteering at my church with student ministries but feeling more and more that I should be doing something else. Our church ministered effectively to children, youth, and older adults, but very few young adults were a part. A church with attendance over 2,000 should probably have more than 20 young adults involved.

The executive pastor asked me to develop a ministry with the college ministry pastor geared toward young adults. I shared my philosophical journey into postmodernism and suggested that the emerging postmodern mindset might require a new approach to this ministry. I agreed to be involved if we could develop the young adult ministry using the new tools and be allowed to explore new approaches.

Terry Majors, the college minister, and I were on the same page about postmodernism. However, rather than being converted to a postmodern point of view, he was a native.

In 1996 we launched a small community group. We met on Sunday mornings with a brief time of fellowship, worship, and study but placed most of our emphasis on building relationships. We spent the majority of our time "sharing life" with people. This was a strategic decision; we sensed that ministry was shifting from performance to relationships. The ministry grew, and we made plans to add a worship gathering.

Early in 1997 Terry and I attended Leadership Network's GenX 2.0 conference at Mount Hermon, California. We were apprehensive because of the conference title. We didn't want to listen to people speaking about generational characteristics (Gen-Xers are dark, pessimistic, untrusting), especially while this huge epistemological storm loomed on the horizon. After the first session I remarked to Terry, "I told you we weren't crazy." Others had recognized the emergence of postmodernity too! The conference was a confirmation to us. We were delighted to find others who were on the same path as we were and to find new resources to help us. We learned about authors like Stanley Grenz, Leonard Sweet, and Lesslie Newbigin. We were introduced to new ministry ideas and models. We came home excited about the future of our work.

We decided to build the ministry as a church within a church instead of a life-stage ministry. We were convinced that the young adults would not outgrow this phase and that increasing numbers of older adults would be adopting a postmodern worldview. We developed the ministry without financial support from our mother church and operated like a separate but integrated congregation (as a church develops a Spanish ministry, for example). We desired to teach the mother church's congregation new expressions of Christianity for this emerging new world. We expected that we would eventually transform the church we were a part of or that we would eventually become a separate church. We felt like pioneer missionaries using missiological skills to develop our approach.

We've been working six years on this project at the time of this writing. The ministry has been extremely successful for our congregation and cultural setting. Though we don't know specifically what the future holds for us, we've emerged so far with an expression of Christianity that works in the postmodern world and is also true to historic Christian faith. The process has changed my life and filled me with hope—a postmodern hope!

Some thoughts have emerged through this process. May they bring you hope as well!

At the core, postmodernity represents a new way to think and categorize our thoughts. The Enlightenment and subsequently the modern worldview first emerged in the 1500s as a response to medieval mysticism. It was appropriate at the time and provided a platform for new investigations and understanding. However the Enlightenment promise to explain all the mysteries of the world failed. Physicists, scientists, psychologists, and philosophers have all recognized that it's impossible to remove all the mystery of our existence.

Modernity marginalized matters of faith and moved them to the sidelines ("Faith is fine for people who need it." "Science and religion must be kept separate.") Christian thought leaders didn't like playing on the sidelines, so they adopted many of the Enlightenment assumptions and accommodated Christian belief to the prevailing epistemology. North American Christianity hitched its wagon to modern assumptions. In many ways North American Christianity appears to be more Cartesian than Christian.

I believer it's time to unhitch the wagon. We need to develop a new expression of Christianity for emerging postmodernism.

Faith and Popular Culture

Faith is back. This must be recognized. Revival of faith is occurring in popular culture, not only in the church. Popular culture is filled with spiritual themes, ideas, and messages. Postmodern seekers do not consider the church as the only place to obtain spiritual resources anymore. The secular-spiritual divide is coming down. With the return of faith, most recognize that God and spirituality cannot be removed from any aspect of life. Faith is no longer marginalized. It's an ideal time for new theological categories and thought.

> *That postmodern turn toward the mystics has yielded one of the most surprising developments in contemporary philosophical and theological thought: the amazing return of religion as the most feared "other" of Enlightenment modernity...The most explosive power in many forms of postmodern thought is the return of the Ultimate repressed by the Enlightenment—the return of religion as a phenomenon demanding new attention, new description, and, of course, new critique.*

—David Tracy [6]

Limitations and Contingency

One of the most significant observations of postmodern thought leaders is the recognition of limitations, especially in language, culture, and conceptual understanding. These limitations make it impossible to claim that we understand completely, accurately, or in an absolute sense. We don't know with certainty; we know with contingency. What we know is contingent on our assumptions about language, about conceptual understanding, and on the cultural setting. This view presents a significant challenge for religious thought leaders because they have used the language of certainty for so long.

I had become used to making proclamations of certainty, so revising my language remains a significant challenge for me. It sounds strange, but I find certainty to be warm and comfortable. I like feeling confident. Admitting my limits and recognizing contingency is cold and scary. I am still passionate about my beliefs, but I recognize my cultural bias and my language games. I'm humbled when I think how small I am before the Creator. Paul expresses this concept in 1 Corinthians 13:12-13: "Now we see but a poor reflection as in a mirror; then we shall see face to face. Now I know in part; then I shall know fully, even as I am fully known."

Recognizing contingency and our limitations is a good thing!

Community

Community has always been a buzzword, but in the postmodern world community is essential. Modernity promotes truth as "the way things really are." Any rational person properly informed of the facts can acquire it. Postmodernity promotes a concept that truth equates to agreements formed in community and only people who participate in a community can obtain truth. Radical autonomy is also in the past.

This understanding of truth will be difficult for many Christians to understand because we have built so much of our apologetic, theology, and models of spiritual formation on the *modern* concept of truth and the *modern* concept of radical individual autonomy.

This new understanding of truth means that you cannot obtain truth if you aren't participating in community.

A new concept of truth has emerged: community equals truth.

Spiritual Formation

One of the most extensive revisions will come in the area of spiritual formation. The primary model of spiritual formation in North American Christianity appears to be a didactic teaching model. The North American Church has committed most of its resources to a variety of classrooms in which people sit and listen to a lecture. This format presumes the lecturer is the learned one and the listener is the unlearned one. The exchange of information transforms the unlearned one. Information is transformational.

In the postmodern world, information is not viewed that way. Information is just information. Too much information is available to people (even biblical information), so it's not valued as much as it is by the modern world. My observations in our community suggest that people consider relationships and experiences to be the primary transformers in their lives. This view doesn't remove information from the spiritual formation matrix. It just devalues it a bit.

We have decided to use our resources to build relationships rather than for exchanging information. We may not build a large lecture hall for a church facility, but we may build multipurpose facilities that can be used as an art gallery, coffee house, theater, and community service center.

We have identified five primary paths that people in our community take in their spiritual formation:

- **Cognitive** Transformation through study of the Scriptures.
- **Contemplative** Transformation through contemplative practices such as meditation and prayer.
- **Ascetic Transformation** through service to others.
- **Expressivist** Transformation through self-expression such as artistry, music, storytelling, acting, and filmmaking.
- **Communitarian** Transformation through shared lives.

These paths are by no means prescriptive—just a meager attempt at describing the paths we have observed in our community. Some of these are actually recovered ancient spiritual formation practices. We integrate all these paths into our spiritual formation structure.

Leadership

I have observed that leadership models are adopted from culture. After World War II military leadership models dominated. Leaders distanced themselves from people because they couldn't let personal feelings interfere with good decisions.

I understand and appreciate these leaders. They were effective at a unique time when the world was fighting tremendous evil. World War II was won at the expense of human life. I will never forget my father-in-law describing the way the military stormed the beaches: 1,000 men hit the beach; 500 died. The next 1,000 men hit the beach; 200 died. The next 1,000 men hit the beach; 100 died. The next wave hit, and they would take the beach. Eight hundred men died taking the beach. A leader couldn't be personally involved with these men and let relationships affect decisions. The men who could make these decisions became heroes and our leadership models. For the Builder generation, many aspired to this style of leadership. Many postwar churches and parachurch organizations adopted it, too.

The Boomers didn't have a mission as noble as their parents. Their parents had defeated Nazism and Communism. So the Boomer mission became advancing the quality of life. The Boomer leaders had a different style. People like Steve Jobs, Michael Eisner, and Bill Gates led by mission. *Mission is king.* The leader is the mission keeper. Many contemporary churches and parachurch organizations have adopted this leadership model in which personal relationships are often sacrificed for the sake of the mission.

Many postmodern people realize how arbitrary mission statements are and fail to see the benefit of making the mission king. The challenge before us is to develop a new leadership model that is effective in building permanent relationships, where relationships are king. My observation of voluntary relational organizations is that leadership is simply a compelling relationship. Postmodern leadership will be extremely important, and we have much to learn about it.

Final Thoughts

I will save other observations about postmodernity, modernity, and the future for another time, but I do want to share my personal feelings— but please remember these are my feelings, and I know how limited I am.

My contention is that modern Christianity has become captive to Western Cartesian rationalism and is having a difficult time freeing itself. We're warned against captivity such as this in Colossians 2:6-8: "So then, just as you received Christ Jesus as Lord, continue to live in him, rooted and built up in him, strengthened in the faith as you were taught, and overflowing with thankfulness. See to it that no one takes you captive through hollow and deceptive philosophy, which depends on human tradition and the basic principles of this world rather than on Christ."

North American Christianity has agreed to the assumptions of the modern world and has built much of its theology, practice, and ministry models with these assumptions. I feel as though Truth died when we agreed to the modern concept of it. North American Christianity has become enamored with Mazlowian motivational theory, and many churches think it noble to proclaim, "We meet people's needs." North American Christianity unknowingly has become empirical, demanding evidence and fact to build faith on. Radical individualism is pervasive, and people think, "It's all about me."

All of this has contributed to what I feel is the great sin of contemporary North American Christianity: the commodification of Christ. We have turned God into a consumer commodity, and religious leaders are the vendors. My sincere prayer is that the postmodern transition will cause a reformation in North American Christianity and that we will learn a new expression of Christianity to present to the world—a simple, humble, relational expression, people sharing life together, recognizing our limitations, and living in faith.

> *The crisis of modernity and postmodernity, the shift from hegemony to perspective, poses questions for the ministry of the church: Have we ourselves enough nerve, freedom, and energy to move beyond the matrix of modernity and its confident, uncritical wholeness to trust concreteness of the text? Have we enough confidence in the biblical text to let it be our fund for counter-imagination? A no to these questions, in my judgment, consigns the church to disappear with the rest of modernity. A yes can be liberating for the church as a transformational body, liberating even for its ministers who **must stand up and imagine.** [emphasis mine][7]*

Benediction

May the peace of God, which passes all understanding, go with you. May your hearts and minds be filled with hope to serve in this emerging new world. May you live courageously in faith. Amen.

Questions

1. Brad's experience brought him to the realization of "how limited we are by our many assumptions and how marginalizing we have become with our theologies." What has your experience been? Have you found postmoderns to be free from these issues?

2. Brad admits to being challenged in revising his language of certainty. Is it possible to completely eradicate it? Do you find value in using language of certainty for any reason?

3. When it comes to experiencing the work of God, how do your experiences in secular settings compare to your experiences in sacred settings? (For Brad, the settings were the shelter and seminary.)

4. Brad states, "Truth equates to agreements formed in community and only people who participate in a community can obtain truth." What's your response to his assertion?

5. Compare the importance of relationships and information in your community of faith. How much overlap do you experience between them? How does your community invest its resources between the two? Should there be a change?

CHAPTER ELEVEN

Shocking, Unexpected Grace
Jay Bakker

AS I WAS GROWING UP, I NEVER THOUGHT OF GOD AS A GOD OF LOVE AND GRACE. Instead he was an eye. The eye in the sky. My dad grew up in a church that had a big eye painted on a wall near the youth room. A huge, staring eye. God's eye. Always watching. Always judging. Underneath the picture, words were painted: *Be careful little feet what you do.* It was enough to scare the hell out of a kid—literally.

That's the kind of God I grew up with. Even though I was raised in the home of the most famous Pentecostal pastor in the country, I didn't know anything about grace or God's accepting love. To me, God was keeping a giant in-the-sky scorecard, so I'd better live up to his standards or get hit on the head with his big ol' bat. I'd better do everything just right, or I was dead meat.

I started hearing the rapture stories when I was about eight years old. Preachers and Sunday school teachers talked a lot about Christ's second coming. Christians watched movies and read books about it—stories about piles of clothes left on the floor once worn by now-raptured Christians, cars crashing because the drivers were taken up, and people who missed the rapture and got their heads cut off because they'd become Christians and wouldn't take *the mark.*

The hype carried into our everyday lives. Credit cards were a prelude to the mark. Prophecies were being fulfilled, and Jesus would be returning any day. I panicked every time I walked into the house and couldn't find my family members. I frantically ran up and down the stairs, looking for somebody…*anybody.* I thought God had come back and taken my mom, dad, and sister—and left me.

I knew all about Jonah ending up in a whale. I knew how everyone had been drowned but Noah and his family. And I heard a lot of questions like, "Will you be ready to meet God?"

I remember one youth worker who was giving a talk and tapping his microphone like a heartbeat: Tap-tap. Tap-tap. Tap-tap. "Are you ready kids?" Tap-tap. Tap-tap. "Ready to meet Jesus?" Then the tapping slowed down. Then it stopped. The heart stopped beating. That person was dead…and had no more hope if he wasn't saved. "Are you ready, kids?"

I was afraid of God. Unbelievably afraid.

My dad and my mom helped start the *700 Club* and the Christian Broadcasting Network (CBN) before launching their own ministry, PTL (which stands for Praise the Lord). Their ministry grew quickly—from one TV show to a whole television network to building a Christian resort, Heritage Village. Other ministries, like a home for pregnant, unwed teens, were launched. In 1986 when I was 11 years old, the world found out that my parents were real—too real.

When the scandal struck, Dad stepped back from PTL. Jerry Falwell stepped in. We were thankful and hopeful, thinking he would help us. But when supporters asked Dad to return to PTL, Jerry wouldn't give it up.

Eventually Dad was sentenced, shackled, and led off to prison.

Dad had given millions of dollars to other ministries and had helped countless Christians get their starts in ministry. He'd championed the causes of many pastors and Christian musicians. But as soon as the trouble started, Dad was a leper to all those he helped.

No wonder ministers keep their sins secret! Once those secrets become public, the ministers aren't forgiven—they're fired! That doesn't make sense to me. The world isn't that harsh. Why is the church so unforgiving? Jesus said the unbelieving world will know Christians by their love for each other. But in reality, when a minister falls, that love ends. That's what I'd seen all my life.

Suddenly I learned that I was a leper, too, just because my last name is Bakker. My friends weren't allowed to play with me anymore. I not only lost my home at Heritage U.S.A. and my security, but I also lost all my friends. I lost my identity. With all my friends gone, I had a tough time figuring out who I was. The only place I found acceptance was with older neighbor kids who partied a lot. They stepped in when the Christians stepped out.

Pretty soon, I wanted to be just like them. I started to dress like them. I started to drink and smoke like them. And I changed my name—from Jamie Charles to Jay.

The Dark Side of Christianity

By the time Dad was sent to prison, I was one angry kid. I couldn't believe that the preacher who was frequently welcomed in the White House was now in the big house. For three months, Mom asked me if I wanted to visit him in Minnesota, but I wouldn't go.

When a pastor falls, people often forget that a whole family is involved. I'd see our faces plastered on tabloid magazines in the grocery store. Worse, I'd see famous ministers preaching on TV against my father and mother. I saw skits that made fun of my family at youth group meetings. Once I visited a youth group where the youth pastor slammed my dad. Later I politely told him who I was and that I didn't appreciate his words. He didn't care. He treated me with disdain. I saw pure hypocrisy and ugliness right then and there, the dark side of Christianity.

Imagine what these experiences did to a young teen who already thinks God is a tyrannical judge!

I was kicked out of school because I was a behavior problem. Besides being an angry 17-year-old, I felt rejected and suffered from dyslexia, a condition not taken seriously at the time.

I left for Minnesota and started to work at a church near the prison my dad was in. I called all the Christian leaders I could think of, asking them to sign petitions to get my dad out of prison and to encourage their congregations to do the same. I didn't have much luck. Many of Dad's closest friends wouldn't even talk to me. Working in the church I was reminded that it was Christ's church, even though I was getting refusals from Dad's "friends"—brothers and sisters in the faith—to help.

I was shocked to find out that Mom was leaving Dad and that Dad's right-hand man was going to marry her.

On the other hand, I began to experience an awesome relationship with Dad. I began to see something in his life as I hung around him. It would be some time before I would understand what it was—grace. Dad was so forgiving of the people who had run him out of the ministry, of his friends who'd deserted him. Even though I didn't have a term for it, I got a peek at what Christianity is supposed to be. It enthralled me.

When my dad was transferred to Georgia, I went also. I was offered a home nearby as long as I went to church every week. That helped me grow closer to Christ, but back among my old friends, I battled with smoking and drinking again, especially drinking. I wouldn't admit I had a problem.

When my father got out of prison, he sent me to Master's Commission, a program for young people planning to go into ministry. I was 18.

A lot of the stuff at the camp seemed irrelevant to my culture, especially since I was dealing with alcohol and cigarette addictions. Everyone else at Masters' Commission seemed like perfect Christians.

A couple of punk kids left Master's Commission to start Revolution, a ministry to street kids. I joined them. We got tattooed to fit in with the people we wanted to help. We prayed three hours a day, but I was still struggling to be a "good Christian." I was petrified that I might sin or make a mistake. Anytime I did, the guy I lived with dressed me down. He had promised me a position in the ministry leadership but didn't give it to me. My act wasn't cleaned up enough, he told me. I wasn't "good enough."

I suddenly learned that legalism doesn't always dress in a suit and tie. It can sport a Mohawk and tattoos.

During the time I worked at the church in Minnesota, I realized Christ had a call on my life. Other people affirmed it. But during the year I spent with Revolution, I felt like a total loser. I returned to Georgia where my friend Donnie Earl Paulk offered me a home. After moving in with the Paulk family, I started drinking again. I was back in that vicious cycle.

Donnie and his family didn't judge me. They didn't have to—I was depressed and overwhelmed enough by my own condemnation. I was eaten up by guilt and couldn't enjoy life. I felt so much pressure: "If I drink, have a lustful thought, or smoke a cigarette, God's going to tell my pastor. God's going to hate me. I *already* feel like God hates me!"

When I finally expressed my thoughts to Donnie, he said something to me I had never heard before: "What are you doing? What are you thinking?

You're making Christ's death be in vain! You're trying to earn your salvation. That's just a bunch of BS."

One night I was out smoking on the porch. When Donnie joined me, he said, "Even if you're out here smoking cigarettes, God still loves you!"

I couldn't believe that God actually loved me. I didn't buy into this grace crap. I responded forcefully, "Prove it to me! I've seen Christianity from all sides. Prove to me that Christ loves me unconditionally!"

Donnie encouraged me to read Paul's letters for myself—Ephesians, Galatians, Romans. Especially Ephesians 2:8-9. We've been saved by grace, not by our own efforts.

Read Paul's letters myself? I'd never actually read the Bible myself! It wasn't rebellion. I simply didn't realize I needed to. The preachers I'd listened to my entire life seemed to have all the answers. They never said, "I might be wrong here. God might be saying something else to you through this Scripture. What is God speaking to your heart?"

The idea of not having to work for my salvation—not having to act a certain way before God accepts me—was intriguing. I started reading about grace and was dumbfounded. It seemed too good to be true—that God loves me, addictions and all. I called my dad to tell him what I'd found. He happily exclaimed, "That's it, son!"

It was the *grand ah-ha!* I had always wished God were more accessible and not just a cosmic traffic cop waiting to ticket me. Then I discovered the shocking secret: God loves me just the way I am.

Grace.

I'd lived in the middle of Christianity all of my life. I'd gone to some of the largest churches in the country. How would I know that God offered such grace when I heard no teaching on God's grace and God's love? When churches and people seldom demonstrate grace? God loves us as we are. He accepts us. We don't have to change to be saved!

I didn't know I could just serve Christ without fulfilling all the church's requirements, but God told me, "I love you regardless of whether you're a minister or an alcoholic your whole life." As I soaked in those words, I started living in freedom. I wasn't worried about the people around me anymore. That's what enabled me to stop drinking. When I was 20 years old, I started going to a 12-step program, not caring what others thought.

You Can't Keep the Good News Down

Eventually I got back into ministry.

Over the last seven years, I've realized that grace is the vital element the church is missing. We'll never be able to fully grasp the concept of being loved no matter how we act, but we must constantly remind ourselves of it. If we don't, legalism creeps in, and we start admonishing, "Don't do this. Don't do that."

Is it any wonder why celebrities like Marilyn Manson, who grew up in Christian homes, often rebel the way they do? When they hit their 20s, 30s, and 40s, they conclude, "The church is fake. I don't want anything to do with it."

And they're right. A whole generation is dying, and we're not relevant. We don't need another sermon about holiness! Martin Luther said teaching justification should be the main focus of our ministries.

Eventually I started working with Revolution in Atlanta just because I wanted to tell people Jesus loves them and accepts them. I couldn't keep that good news to myself. I felt compelled to get the message of grace to the people who needed to hear it.

A lot of people freaked, asking, "Are you giving license to sin?"

Not at all. But you can't expect everybody to get it. They don't see freedom in Christ. They see the conditional love I saw my whole life. The sad thing is that we, the church, have the only thing that's real, but we've cloaked it with tradition and our own ideas. We've watered it down until the gospel we're preaching is a humanistic gospel. But we have something so beyond that! Jesus has love and passion for us!

Jesus' love for us doesn't mean we'll be perfect. Look at the ministers who fall. I think one reason my dad fell was because he was placed on such a high pedestal. He was expected to be perfect. But Jesus never used perfect people; Jesus hung out with prostitutes and tax collectors.

Look at the story of the prodigal son. Although the good son never left home, his good works and pride kept him from truly coming into his father's presence. In the same way, our good works can keep us away from God.

Bad works are blatant in the world. When you're in sin, you need God. But when you're caught up with man's religion, you think you have it all together. Before Paul was converted, he was so religious that he killed people whom he judged as heretical. But talk about grace! Paul, a murderer and legalistic Pharisee, ended up writing a huge part of the New Testament.

Grace is for everybody—the prostitute on the street and the legalistic minister in the pulpit. Taking out your earrings, promising not to date, filling out forms, those have nothing to do with salvation. So many kids have been kicked out of our churches for those very transgressions. You know what happens when we kick people out? We're *really* saying, "You're not good enough." We send a message that Jesus' death wasn't enough to bring them to God.

The truth is, none of the disciples—or even Jesus for that matter—could make it through a youth program today based on the requirements some churches set up. Rather than settling for bodybuilders tearing phone books in half and lighting pyrotechnics at big youth rallies, we need to be saying to kids, "We'll love you no matter what."

Man's religion can be devastating and condemning, but Jesus says, "Come as you are." In fact, those in the Lutheran church are careful to say we *receive* Christ, not we accept Christ. I love that because grace is all about what Jesus does for us. We don't do anything. We just receive what he gives us. Jesus relentlessly pursues us to give us grace.

Grace is awesome! Grace keeps no record of wrongs. It endures through every circumstance. Grace is for real people. We get further with grace than we ever will with the dramatics the church uses so much.

We live under such an amazing God, but the message of his unconditional love and unending grace is often lost. That's part of the reason why I don't think we'll ever be able to truly grasp that we're completely forgiven.

A Face to Grace

One of the greatest lessons I've learned in ministry is to recognize when I'm wrong. I can be wrong, and I can be corrected. You can be wrong, and you can be corrected. My favorite band, Social Distortion, has a song called, "I Was Wrong." That's also the title of my dad's book. We have a hard time admitting when we're wrong, but when we've made a mistake, we should admit it and move on. We should be humble, even though being humble hurts. You learn by failing, but it's not fun.

After I started learning about grace and my freedom in Christ, I had to learn to forgive and show grace to others. Dad showed me the way. He brought a face to grace that I'd never seen before. Dad has ministers over to his house all the time—people he forgave for hurting him. I used to tell my dad, "That guy's a jerk. Why are you talking to him?" But Dad wanted to live out grace.

Soon enough I learned that if I'm going to live in freedom, too, I had to learn how to forgive. My unforgiving attitude and bitterness felt like a ball and chain—a thousand balls and chains.

Recently an incident occurred that I should have confronted in love. I was cooking on the inside, so I let the sun go down on my wrath. After a huge argument, I realized how much the waiting had cost me in the long run. We're working the problem out, but it could have—should have—gone differently. I should have been more open, more forgiving, and more ready to demonstrate grace. I've been working on that lately in my life—but it's not easy. Like I said, humility is not fun.

Studying for the Bar Exam

If you want to deal with people on a real level, go to a bar.

Every Monday night I go to an English pub. I've gotten to know the people there. They've become my close friends, and I've earned their trust. It took time for them, but in some way, I've impacted their lives.

Once I mentioned it would be cool if they put Social Distortion in the jukebox. When I came back the next time, the songs I liked were in the jukebox. To me, that shows they care about me. I'm part of their lives.

I've learned not to worry about what other Christians say about me. If no Christian would receive me ever again, I would still go to bars, to those areas where I can get to know the people who need grace. I'd do it even if I didn't have ministry credentials.

My pub friends see Christians handing out tracts on the street all the time. They see it as incredibly eerie; it makes them uncomfortable. They say to me, "They're telling us we're sinners and going to hell. See? That's why I'd never be a Christian."

That kind of evangelism makes the *Christians* feel better, not the people they pray for. To me it's a cop-out. Scripture says God won't raise his voice in the streets or snuff out the smallest hopes.[1]

The church has to get back to being more practical and offering the radical message of grace. It's not always easy to live by grace. I've come a long way from not knowing grace existed to finally seeing the light, but I'm far from where I need to be. Grace isn't always popular in churches that are uncomfortable with people who don't fit into its molds. People who live in grace may not look like *us*.

Grace is the whole reason Jesus died! Grace is the ultimate freedom. We can't give our lives to teaching anything less.

"Amazing grace, how sweet the sound." I've learned it's true. So true.

Questions

1. Does the church encourage us to be afraid of God? How is this different from fearing God?

2. Have you experienced "the grand ah-ha" in your life? What prevented you from realizing God's unconditional love for you? Or what prevents you from accepting it now? How is life different when you recognize God's unconditional love for you?

3. In your experience, are churches unforgiving toward leaders who sin? How should fallen leaders be dealt with?

4. What do you think about holding leaders to a higher moral standard than the rest of the body of Christ? What about their family members? How can you live more grace-fully with them?

5. Jay's father "brought a face to grace" for him. How can you be a face to grace for people you encounter?

CHAPTER TWELVE

Emerging from the Water
George R. Baum

"REMEMBER YOUR BAPTISM."

This always perplexed me. It was the Lutherans around me who told me to remember that day—and that's what made it all so weird, since these people knew quite well I was a life-long Lutheran and couldn't possibly remember the events of February 1964, even with the most aggressive regressive therapy.

Still, the reminder came, "Remember your baptism."

The *affirmation* of my baptism (or confirmation) I could remember. The youth group paper drives I could remember. The insanely bright orange color we painted the youth room I could remember. But my baptism? Couldn't remember it. Couldn't remember my pastor's weekly sermons either, though I developed an impression of what they were about. Whether accurate or not, my impression of what was important to my pastor was that I should remember to behave.

It seemed to me that what folks really wanted to see in my relationship with God was good behavior. Doing the right thing didn't seem to be related to any earthly rewards (other than the obvious ability to sit down comfortably), but I was struck deep with the notion that God wanted me to behave. As a youngster in Sunday school—that cookie and punch time—this behavior stuff took the form of Sometimes People Do Bad Things, but Jesus Loves Us Anyway. Gradually the lesson learned was Sometimes People Do Good Things if They Try Really Hard. Through high school the message was more focused: Don't Drink, Don't Smoke, Don't Have Sex. Oh, and as always, through it all, Remember Your Baptism. It seemed a strange collection of lessons to have gathered from a childhood among the Lutherans. But all these lessons I put inside my Sack O' Faith, confident that I'd find what I needed for my journey if I ever dug around in there.

So I journeyed on. I traveled through the stages of enthusing at youth camp, experimenting by inviting the Mormons over for coffee, and evolving into a fellow who wasn't sure all this religious stuff really made sense. I trudged forward, living my life, secretly hoping that the time would never come when I'd actually need to use the stuff I carried in my

Sack O' Faith. After all, I wasn't sure what was in it, and I surely didn't know how to use whatever I might find if I dared to dig around in that Sack O' Faith. After all, who could make sense of this stuff? I carried around various stories of Old Testament heroes mixed up with stories of New Testament radicals mixed up with the important stuff like don't drink and don't smoke. I knew that a steady keel and a firm conviction to avoid the sinful things of this world would protect me from ever needing to look inside that sack. As long as things were going well, I would never need to figure out what I really believed.

Eventually, though, I needed to step out on my own. College was calling —though I was on the other line. I started a career flipping eggs at Denny's and playing local bands at night. No tragedy in sight, no need to dig around in the Sack O' Faith. People died in the proper order. People were punished for misbehaving by local law enforcement. Life was making some sense as I moved away from the faith of my childhood. I was slowly escaping from a senseless collection of cookies-and-punch stories and becoming a man who wasn't sure God existed at all.

In October 1991, my youngest brother John called on the phone to say he'd received test results that concluded he was HIV-positive. The Journalism 101 questions began to spill out or at least flood into my mind. Who? What? How? When? And mostly, *why?* I assured my brother that I would do anything and everything for him; he only needed to ask me. We flew him out for visits. We argued with insurance companies and doctors. We organized a stunning regimen of drugs and tests. The virus marched onward, undaunted by our actions. John was going to die, and nothing anybody did would stop that.

I loved my brother. I was facing more than a crisis of faith; I was facing a crisis of life itself. Could I live in a world without my brother? Could I live at all? It seemed odd to ask myself those questions, and I kept them to myself.

A friend of mine, whom I'll call Karl, is a man of great faith commitment. Karl is not known for emotional displays nor is he given to half-hearted or untested faith statements. One night, over dinner, Karl confronted me with the need to confront my brother about his homosexuality. In Karl's view, my brother's time on earth was limited, and since Karl knew of my love for my sibling, he argued that the most loving thing I could do is walk John to the door of repentance for his sinful life.[1]

I must say, I was frightened, confused, and angry, mainly at the prospect that Karl might be right. Was this how my final days with John would be spent? By cajoling, confronting, and condemning? I had planned to spend my days comforting John, helping him walk confidently to the door of death. If Karl was right, not only was I going to lose my brother, I was also going to lose our relationship for what little remained of his life. A young gay man, who felt betrayed by the church of his childhood, wasn't going to repent to please me. In John's view, the church didn't want him hanging around, and he wasn't going to give us the pleasure of telling him so to his face. He avoided the church, and the church didn't seem to mind that arrangement.

But now, with Karl's bringing things down to basic truths, I was facing a stunning crisis of faith, because there was no way I could embrace a God whose only concern for my dying, suffering, beloved brother was that John repent. If that was the nature of God, I was not all that interested. My life was being ripped apart, and I had no time for judgment and faultfinding. What to do about my brother's plight occupied all my attention. My brother was slipping away before my eyes. I needed to assure him of…of something.

What message did I have for my brother? Don't drink? Try really hard? Remember your baptism? None of these fine upstanding messages was going to be much help. I needed something bigger, something more lasting, something a beloved brother dying far too young might take on his journey into the hereafter. As I looked in my bag of religious phrases and philosophies I came up empty.

I thrashed about my religious life, looking for comfort, both for myself and for John. The main thing I could think to tell him was that not every Christian hates gays. For example, I reasoned. There's me, right? This made sense to John. In fact, I recall him saying "Yes, but you're my brother. These other people don't care about me at all." And I think he might've been right. To be sure, while they cared a great deal about his homosexual orientation, his value as a person seemed open to debate.

For my own part, the assurance that I wasn't John's enemy wasn't exactly the magic, life-giving message of the gospel I'd heard so much about. I finally made up my mind to do the one thing that made sense to me: I loved my brother with all my heart, and I told him so as often as either of us could bear. Maybe that eased his journey. I hope it did. One day I want to remember to ask him, though I suspect we'll have other things on our minds.

On August 20, 1994, John David Baum breathed his last. I spoke with him—or, actually to him—in his final hours, explaining that my wife, Cris, and I would be on a plane from Los Angeles in a few hours and we'd be there soon. At his bedside in the hospital were my parents and Father Pirelli, John's counselor and confessor at AIDS Family Services. Though Cris and I did get on the first flight, John's body could not hold out. He was gone before we landed. I took comfort in Father Pirelli's assurances that John did have a strong faith, but it was a private faith. They had prayed together often, and John found our loving God in a place where the church proper forgot to tell him to look.

With the death of my brother, I entered a time of great darkness. Not a time of searching, not a time of looking for meaning, not a silent acceptance of the cycles of life. Just darkness, thorough and complete. Looking back on it, it seems like it was someone else's life. My life was full of all sorts of things that are the very goals in life. I was blessed with a wife who knew me well and (yet somehow) loved me unconditionally. Together, we were blessed with a beautiful daughter, who was born three months before John's death. My musical career was beginning to take shape, and I was making a comfortable living. Everything was in place for a life of happiness. And yet, I was stuck in the midst of the valley of the shadow of death: John's death.

In an effort to make me comfortable, people threw bumper-sticker theology at me. Short little phrases meant to bring comfort to the afflicted. We've all heard them. Maybe in our struggle to bring comfort we've even found ourselves saying such things. People would tell me, "The Lord knows best." Or, "Your brother's happier now because he's worshiping at the throne of God." Or, "God needed a flower for his garden."

When I'd hear these thoughtless, heartless "encouragements," the only thing that kept my blood from boiling was the chill up my spine. Had these people never experienced such devastating loss? Had they never spent time in this valley of darkness?

I began to assume I'd spend the rest of my life in that valley. What was making it all the more horrific was that I was alone in the middle of a crowd. I couldn't be comforted with the thought that I'd one day escape and find the people outside the valley. The incomprehensible truth was that my valley was right in the thick of everyone else's lives. All around me, events were going as one expects and wants them to go. Life was good, but I wasn't actually living. I couldn't possibly explain this bizarre contradiction to anyone, not even my wife. I was a zombie of some sort, and I settled in for the long haul of never recovering from my brother's death.

Around this time, Cris and I began attending St. Thomas Episcopal Church in Los Angeles. This is a congregation made up, for the most part, of young gay males. It seemed a place of comfort for me at that time and was most certainly a place that would've brought comfort to John. Many of the parishioners had died of AIDS or were in the process of doing so.

This was the place where I first encountered the bumper sticker-length phrase that finally brought some comfort. When praying for the departed in the Book of Common Prayer, in several versions of the prayers of the people, there's the phrase, "For those whose faith was known only to you." The first time I read it, I began to weep uncontrollably and carried our infant daughter to the narthex on the pretext that she was crying. I remember that morning quite clearly, because I sensed a faint shaft of light in my huge, dark valley. That prayer put into words what I'd known in my heart all along. My brother was a man of faith. I knew it; John knew it; John's priest and counselor who walked him to death's door knew it. But the church prevented John from acting on his faith publicly. Or rather, John did not feel welcome in the community of faith, so his faith was known only to God.

As for myself, I was still living in darkness, but I wasn't alone. God had somehow joined me in that dark valley. The rest of the phrase from

Psalm 23 caught up with me. I was walking in the valley of the shadow of death, but God met me there and comforted me. Still, I was at a loss to explain all this to other people. Time was passing, and everyone was expecting me to get on with life. One isn't supposed to grieve forever, you know. I trudged along, functioning normally but suffering deeply.

As I was all too aware, nothing was in my Sack O' Faith to help me during this life-threatening crisis. I didn't even bother looking into those lessons. I turned outward, through reading, hoping someone else might share my loneliness. I stumbled on the writings of Robert Capon. His writing made sense to me and allowed that John would be welcomed by a fully redeeming and unconditionally loving God.

I was still in that dark valley, but now God and Robert Capon were with me. I wondered, "Will others be joining me or will I eventually be leaving?" It didn't much seem to matter. As far as I could tell, I had no control over my fate. I would sit and wait it out. Then, about five books into his writings, I came to Capon's own description of my plight. More accurately, Capon was describing how he escaped from this same valley.

It came with a simple realization: you can't blame a corpse for being dead.

I was alive, and to all outside observers, I was functioning fine, but I was a corpse, a walking, breathing, fully functioning corpse. The way Robert Capon describes it, once he realized he was a corpse, he was set free. I cannot possibly explain why this notion brought me comfort, but it most certainly did. I knew and was experiencing exactly what he described. Unable to find someone who understood, we had each become dead, a walking corpse, filled with the guilt of not being able to bring himself back to life.

That's where the miracle comes in. Only by accepting my deadness was I able to release myself from the blame of being dead. The notion that people can't blame a corpse for being dead brought freedom from guilt.

The oddest thing about this experience was that the first step to freedom and life was to recognize that I was, in fact, dead. It's the inability to accept one's own powerlessness that gets in the way here. You see your arms and legs move. You hear yourself talking. You even fancy yourself thinking and feeling. But deep inside, you know that you are as dead as any corpse in a coffin, and you can't do a thing to raise yourself up out of that deep, dark grave. Coming to grips with that strange notion, one can be brought back to life by trusting in the One who can do something about this death experience.

It doesn't make sense, does it? Of course not. But to those of us who have been there, this realization is the *only* thing that makes sense. Safely dead, I began to pray again. Knowing that I was not responsible for being dead, I began to trust once more that God truly loved me. Rather than seeing my death as darkness, it was becoming a source of freedom.

As it turns out, it was okay to be dead, provided I was willing to trust that God could resurrect me. And since I had no hope of hauling myself out of the grave, trusting in God's power was my only option. Jesus had been through this valley, as had Lazarus.

It was the story of Lazarus to which I clung, for many reasons. First and foremost, Lazarus didn't bring himself out of the grave. Nobody blamed him for being dead, though they did sort of blame Jesus, I suppose. But all Lazarus did was die and then come out when Jesus called.

Second, in this story Jesus speaks what has become my personal theme verse. "Jesus said to Martha, 'Your brother will rise again.' " (John 11:23). Even my simple mind can remember its location, since my brother's name was John, and my birthday is 11/23. I take that as my personal verse of hope. For me, if that one's true, then the whole thing can be true. And I'm willing to stake my fortunes on the words of the Word. After all, he seems to know about life and death, doesn't he?

Back in the valley, I was slowly putting my life back together. I had the rare opportunity to essentially rebuild my faith life from scratch. Where to begin? I started back with what I knew for certain. I had been baptized. God had claimed me as a child and nothing could separate me from God's love. So I had my starting point upon which I'd rebuild this stuff.

In clinging to that starting point, you know what I was doing? Remembering my baptism! Yep, it had been there the whole time, along with the key to actually using it. But until I needed to take this hard look at what I believed, I'd never needed to remember my baptism. Those Lutherans knew what they were talking about. It became clear to me that—in the midst of this faith crisis and death itself—only the rebirth of the waters of baptism could give me a fresh start.

The second step was seeking out the gospel. I never had to look for the law. It was everywhere. If I ever thought I might not be hearing it, a visit from a professional Christian speaker might bring the law crashing down. Plenty of law to go around, thank you very much. The most extreme example of the law's pervasiveness is that I felt *guilty* for being dead. I mean, if that isn't a seeming final victory for the law, what is? Yet I knew—and know—that the gospel is out there. In fact, it's everywhere too; sometimes one has to look for it. And look for it I do.

That's because, it turns out, I need the gospel. It's honestly the only thing holding me up most days. Everything else was stripped away back in the valley of the shadow of death. I found I could only understand the gospel when it was the only thing I had.

Since I've seen what the gospel can do, I know its value. I seek it out, I point it out, and I shout it out. This gospel must be heard, because there are dead people walking among us. You may know some of them, or you may be one of them. It's nothing to be ashamed of. In fact, it's probably a great opportunity to meet this life-giving God without distraction. You just have to be willing to accept that you're dead, and there's only one way you're going to get "not dead." As any psychologist will tell you, the first step to recovery is to admit you need help. The only difference is, you and I need help every day. Putting the old Adam to death, remembering our baptism, and accepting new life in Jesus Christ. Simple concept, hard to pull off, eh?

> When we were baptized into Christ Jesus, we were baptized into his death. We were therefore buried with him through baptism into death, in order that, just as Christ was raised

from the dead through the glory of the Father, we too might live a new life. If we have been united with him like this in his death, we will certainly also be united with him in his resurrection.

—adapted from Romans 6:3-6

That's what Paul says. It fits my own experience, I must say. Perhaps what I mean is, in order for me to live my life, I have to accept that I am dead and be born again. Hmmm…whoever seeks his life will lose it, and whoever loses his life shall find it? No, that must just be something I heard in a sermon somewhere. It couldn't really be true, could it?

Not only *could* it be true, it is true. I'm living proof of that. Remember my baptism. Remember John's baptism. Remember your baptism. Someday you might find that you need to. And what, you ask, does all this have to do with ministry?

Everything!

I've learned that, in matters of faith, it's okay to say, "I don't know." There was a time, when I considered it my duty to have a scriptural, theological, exegetical response for every question anyone ever asked. Somehow I'd gotten the notion that this was my Christian duty. But that kind of thinking leads us to be afraid of having conversations about Jesus. I mean, what if someone asks a question I don't have an answer for? What if someone is mad at God for the pain in her life? Plenty of theologians have weighed in on such issues over time, but those treatises don't necessarily help in the midst of suffering. If a young person asks how a caring God could let a loved one die a tragic death, it probably doesn't help to hand her a lengthy position paper on the consequences of the Fall.

I've found that in having to say, "I don't know," it naturally follows to simply be there for people. To say, "I'm not sure," and follow it up with, "but I'll wait here with you," reflects the love of a God who cares. In the incarnation of Jesus, God says he will be with us in the midst of our suffering. In a life filled with senseless pain, having God shedding tears by your side makes it all more bearable. Our God is a God who joins people in their valleys of suffering. I know first hand that it makes all the difference in the world.

Questions

1. What feelings or memories surface as you remember your baptism?

2. What's in your Sack O' Faith that shapes the Christian you are today?

3. Put yourself in George's place as he struggled to find the best way to minister to his dying brother. What would you have done in his situation?

4. What was the darkest time in your life? In what specific ways did God minister to you during that time? What drew you out of your valley?

5. What could help the church be better equipped to minister to people who are dead in the same way that George was dead?

6. Do you find yourself avoiding conversations about Christ with others in crisis because you think you have to have answers to their questions? How does an answer-driven witness hinder spiritual renewal in others?

CHAPTER THIRTEEN

Faith That Matters in the Culture of Ghosts
Parush R. Parushev

I WAS BORN IN BULGARIA SHORTLY AFTER THE END OF WORLD WAR II, into a family of fanatic believers for several generations. As with many others of this kind, my father and grandfather were sent to the gulags and prisons because of their beliefs.

It happened to be that my family fanatically believed in the ideals of Communism. They committed their lives to it and were absolutely sure that what they were doing was right. In their understanding, this was the best way of life, both for a person and the society. They—and later I as well—were hoping for and working toward the coming of the "bright future," a future of the Communist society that would solve the problems of suffering and injustice for all people. They did not doubt for a second that the Ghost of Communism that Marx and Engels had envisioned in the *Communist Manifesto* was coming and indeed was already there. Their commitment to the vision was so consuming that they were ready to sacrifice their lives to bring that bright future closer.

Where is this bright future today? Its vision collapsed in the late 1980s, and, as in Matthew 7, the collapse was a great one.

For me the seemingly firm structure of my Communist convictions cracked and collapsed 10 years earlier, with a realization that there was another equally valuable viewpoint and equally fanatic people ready just the same to sacrifice their lives for their convictions. I had no doubts about the purpose of my life until I encountered a group of Christian believers. I didn't even think they still existed!

I met them, Roman Catholic believers, in Krakow, Poland, a country I happened to visit early in my carrier as a scientist. They brought to my attention a reality of faith. They lived their lives differently simply because they believed in God. These people forced me to think hard and to look back on my life and the moral shape of the Communist society. I had to admit they made better sense of their moral living. This was the beginning of where I am now, some 20 years later.

Going after a Ghost

Before going into some details of these 20 years, let me share a piece of witness that concerns a certain Orthodox priest, Father George Florovski. Those of us who come from the Orthodox communities know him, since he is one of the three most influential figures of 20th-century Orthodox theological thinking—together with Fathers Schmemann and Meyendorff.[1] In a conversation at Harvard Divinity School in the late 1950s, a student asked Father Florovski about how he became a believer. He answered this way: "My father, also an Orthodox priest, initiated me, without compulsion, into the mysteries of faith."[2]

Two positive (and one negative) conditions surface in this short testimony that are illustrative of the formation of our convictions. First, one has to be initiated. Some give witness to their belief by the integrity of their life. For Father Florovski, the members of his family, by their lives, initiated him into faith.

Second, faith has a quality of mystery. It can't be expressed in words alone. Surely an intellectual dimension of certain concepts can be summarized, yet it can't be exhausted by concepts. Faith leaves open a wide range of mysterious expressions that aren't verbalized and can't be put into doctrines. Faith in Christ and new life in Christ are mysteries—tangible, yet mysteries.

As for the negative condition in the Father's testimony, faith does not come by compulsion or force. There is no such thing as a forced faith. No faith is an inherited faith. Much of the confusion today in Eastern Europe comes from the political arrangements of Christendom that require national identity and religious affiliation to coincide. For Father Florovski, however, to truly believe, you have to be free from compulsion. You have to experience the supernatural, to see it present and making a difference in the lives of others. Any faith has some objective roots. Unless something of the envisioned is present, nothing will lead your will into making a faith commitment.

Reading Father Florovski's testimony for the first time, I was struck by its similarity to my testimony as a Communist. I was initiated into

Communism by my family. I became a Communist because I saw the integrity of the belief in the lives of two generations of Communists. Everyone in my family was a committed Communist. I was surrounded by good and caring people who initiated me into their faith in a way similar to Father Florovski's initiation into his. And this faith was equally mysterious. We believed in an immediately unforeseeable future that would be brighter than the present. We were led to that future by an invisible and mighty Party that demanded all our allegiance. I chose to become a Communist when I was 20 years old, convinced that this was the right way of life. I was not forced to do that; I came to the point of believing in the Communist ideals myself. What made my commitment even stronger was the fact that I could see and participate in the attempts to materialize the dream.

What is the difference, then, between one raised in a Communist family and initiated into the Communist way of life by parents who lived their lives with integrity, and one brought into a Christian family, having witnessed the Christian lifestyle and having been initiated into the Christian faith? Do these two differ in any significant way? Does one form of religious belief essentially differ from all the others?

Existentially, I don't see much difference. Each of us has our hopes and beliefs; we don't differ much in the way we hold to one set of convictions or another. To determine the difference, you have to look further than yourself, your home, and your nuclear family. You have to look at the community holding the same beliefs—if there is such a community. Then you can compare the impact this community makes on the lives around it.

This is how, upon meeting those Polish believers, it occurred to me that something might be wrong with the beliefs of my family. Although two generations before me were ready to die for their beliefs, Communism still wasn't enough to regenerate the lives of others. In fact, the moral life of the socialist society I was living in was degenerating every year. This was when, for the first time, I realized that the community's witness matters as much as our personal witness—or even more. I thought that as Communists we possessed the right philosophy of life. We taught it in schools. We proclaimed it through the media. We had it published in doctrines and statements forced on everyone. But right teaching could not guarantee nor even launch right living in the community. Unfortunately, this sad lesson can be learned from the history of the Christian church, too.

The more I think about the fateful days of December 1980, the more I value the inspiration and the vision of a community of people who dare to live them out. The contrast between the life of a community moving forward by their vision and another community sinking in desperation because of a faded vision, was striking. Verbalized concepts of their faith in God weren't what caught me. I don't even remember them talking about that. What fascinated me were the obvious signs of something elusive yet real that these people possessed and were bound together by—something I didn't have.

We can't help but respect a person with integrity of character, even if we may not agree with this person's beliefs. But what really impresses us and takes us by surprise is a *community* with integrity of character. This is what I experienced in my encounter with that local Polish Roman Catholic community. Their communal faithfulness put my beliefs to the test and later played a significant role in subverting the whole framework of the political system I believed in. Faced with the powerful witness of these people, I was forced to examine "unquestionable truths" I took for granted.

Slowly and painfully I realized that what I believed to be a well-grounded, logical, rational philosophy of life turned out to be a religion.[3] As with any other religion, it was founded on the "uncontested truth" of the holy narratives of the founders: Marx, Engels, Lenin, and others. A caste of party secretaries was set aside to interpret the texts for the public. A set of true doctrines was derived from those texts. They were systematized and enforced as the only right teaching. Any rival religious group was condemned and suppressed. New party members were conducted into the privileged group through special rituals of initiation. The holy shrines, the icons, and the statues of the founders and saints of Communism were visited and venerated. Psalmodies of hymns were created to praise the achievements of the Party and the glorious future. Processions and pilgrimages of the faithful with banners of the saints past and present—the members of the Politburo—were periodically organized.

Human history records numerous attempts to fulfill the dream of Christendom—the Kingdom of God on earth. The Communist society was the last, and perhaps the most aggressive, attempt to realize the vision. This was the Kingdom that banned the King. Instead, an impersonal and almighty Party was demanding the allegiance of the Kingdom's subjects in the name of an earthly paradise. The incredible power of this vision was sustained partly by the perverse assurance of the supremacy of human reason and partly by the appeal to egalitarian sameness of each and every individual.

Watching that community of Polish believers, I had to admit that religious beliefs are expressed first and foremost in the moral life of its adherents. The real crisis for me came when I realized that the Communist religion corrupted, rather than improved, the morality it inherited from the Judeo-Christian culture. Communist ideology claimed to be a supreme expression of secularist and humanist rationality. Perhaps it was true; but it was also true that it was morally deficient on its own terms. This was my foremost concern, having observed the obvious degradation of communal moral values such as family, honesty, integrity, inclusion, and mutual care.

Nothing preoccupied the masterminds of the Communist ideology as much as the subversion of traditional values of kinship, communal relationships, and national identity. The eruptions of numerous bloody conflicts in the former countries of the Communist block are signs of the struggle to recover suppressed communal identity. Called to solve the dilemmas of alienation, Communist society alienated its subjects from each other to a disastrous degree. Almost as in the biblical narrative, allegiance had to be given completely and totally to the Party and its members. "Whoever...does not hate father and mother, wife and children, brothers and sisters—yes, even life itself..." (Luke 14:26, TNIV) The formative story of Communist faithfulness taught to the young generation of the "Soviet peoplehood" was the story of a young pioneer, Pavlik Morozov, who was praised for handing over his parents for death, in obedience to Party orders.

All these memories come to my mind to confirm two points. One is to say that fanatics can be found among any religious breed. Readiness to sacrifice one's life for one's religious beliefs may fascinate, but it rarely convinces. The other is that, whether you want it or not, the life of the community taken by a certain religious vision is the only discernible proof of the moral value of this religion.

Then which community? What religious beliefs?

Several years passed before I was able to sort out answers to those questions and these: Why is Christianity hated so much by my fellow Communist ideologists? Why isn't life in our Communist societies disturbed much by the Orthodox church or Protestant communities, while the Polish Roman Catholics are visible, outspoken, and courageous? To be sure, I was perplexed and fearful of the rigid institutional structure of the Catholic Church that was mirrored too closely by the Communist party structures. At the same time I was impressed by the lives of the Roman Catholics, my colleagues and friends.

Even with these questions still in my mind, one thing was certain: for me Marx's ghost was a ghost indeed.

Finding the Ghost

In a peculiar way, I was disadvantaged in searching for religious meaning. For one thing, I was surrounded by Communists with integrity. In addition, my trained scientific mind appreciated the appealing rationality of secularist and humanist arrangements of the Communist ideology and was very suspicious of logically unsound truths. It required almost 10 years before I was able to come to terms with the profound depth and legitimate reality of religious experience. After the agonizing search was over, the emerging hope in the possibility of "a still more excellent way" (1 Corinthians 12:31, NASB) was all the more exciting. This hope became visible through a community of people who shared their Christian vision and its promises with my wife, our family, and me.

By God's grace, my wife, also a scientist and party member, and I somehow made our way to the radical communities of the Baptists and Pentecostals. I'm still pondering this puzzle, but my guess is that in a desperate, secularist, fragmented society the most appealing communities are the ones that provide a warm, welcoming embrace and emotional fulfillment in which sharing in the lives of others is part of daily living. (Later I realized that much of the attraction to cults in the West is because of the promise to meet these needs for disillusioned individuals in an affluent culture.)

Something new entered our life. It began with a real conversion experience out of which came the sense that a new reality, not human-made, was emerging. We encountered the presence of a Ghost who was real, the Holy Spirit of God himself. In the world around us—about to fall apart—that presence was bringing new meaning into our lives, with wholeness, joy, and fulfilling hope. We were reading the biblical stories into our lives. Taken by that vision, at that time we thought "the more excellent way" was without pitfalls. We still had to grasp that Christian faithfulness is a life of continuous conversion.

Conversion calls for commitment. It flowed naturally from our former convictions. I must give credit to the Communist emphasis on commitment and the demands they put on a person's life: a faithful person was faithful by deeds, not by dreams. This conviction did not allow us to celebrate and rejoice in the solitude of a newly found meaning. We were eager to get involved in the practices of the church life. We soon found ourselves wholeheartedly engaged in the complexity of life in the emerging Baptist communities of our country. Our experience paralleled the prophet Isaiah's (Isaiah 6) and can be summarized in a sentence: whenever God finds you, God calls you, and whenever you respond to God, God sends you. It may sound like a cliché, but for us it is a way of life.

It was an invigorating period, a period of rapid development of local churches, with the flow of spiritually hungry, disillusioned people seeking the meaning of life as we did. They were drawn into the churches by the search for the presence of the Holy that all of us were missing for so long. However, I was sad to see so many of them stumbling over the almost illiterate, primitivist, legalistic pastoral teaching.

I had another lesson to learn: the faithful moral living was of utmost importance for the credibility of the Christian witness, and yet during the end of the 20th century, the intellectual credibility, the artistic, the dramatic, the beautiful, mattered no less. This was what set my wife and me on the track of theological education. For one thing, the gift of teaching, obviously invested in us by God and already tested in our years of academic advancement, was discerned and appreciated by our community. But most importantly, at that very moment, education was one of the most acute needs of the church, and it had to be met.

Pursuing theological education, we were brought into close contact with Western Christianity. During my academic career, I had spent extensive time in the European West, yet the life of the Western church was totally new to me and my wife. North America is a magnet that attracts not only a multitude of immigrants, but also theologians from all over the world. Many of them, unfortunately, never get back to those who so desperately need them. This trend will last for a while, however good or bad that may be—but it's already beginning to change.

So we were among the many seeking theological education in the United States in the early 1990s. Back in school, these were amazing years for us. A new world of intense theological reflections, meaningful inquiries into the biblical texts, and the new multifaceted life of American churches completely filled our life. We were fortunate to be embraced again by a church community that called itself *a family of faith*. And it was that.

In these first years we experienced the blessings of belonging. All the advantages of being immersed in cherished academic activity and being loved and cared for so much turned out to be a disadvantage for us. We indiscriminately transferred our experience to all the Christian communities in the United States.

Being a curious case of converted Communists as well as two of the few international students in the seminary, we had the privilege of traveling to visit different churches and talk with various religious communities. It's difficult to summarize our experiences with them, but after some time passed, we realized that our community was in a sense exceptional. We saw big churches functioning much like a theater. Entertainment and emotional stimulation mattered more than fellowship and involvement. We went to small churches, which were completely preoccupied with doctrinal purity and internal fights and slowly dying. We heard confessions from pastors who were frustrated and depressed because they had purposely distanced themselves from church members out of fear of being too involved. They were acting as employed religious professionals rather than genuine members of the community. We didn't lose our confidence in the Spirit of God, but we began to wonder how ghostly the Spirit can be in a church.

Imparting the Ghost

For some time, we were blind to the undercurrents in our church's and seminary's denomination. When more than 90 percent of the seminary faculty left because of their unwillingness to compromise their integrity with the demands of the new power structure of the denomination, it took us by surprise. We were faced with the grim reality of power plays, dominance, and drives for public and political exposure similar to the ones we always associated with our Communist past.[4] A fellow Russian student expressed his frustration: "We have run away from the Communist past to find that the Bolsheviks are already on the campus!"

At that time, I already knew that education was not knowledge alone. There is something much deeper in the whole idea of learning—first and foremost, trust and personal relationships. You may be taken in by someone's encyclopedic knowledge, but, in the long run, you will follow a teacher with integrity. And this is how I followed the exodus: people drew me to themselves with the integrity of their character. The next stop in my academic pilgrimage was a respected evangelical seminary in California.

Obviously, denominational leadership attempted to enforce ecclesial discipline on the academic community. I realized this was not a challenge faced specifically by this denomination. Something in the air was prompting a shift or division, something that I didn't understand at that moment. I was aware that something new was emerging in churches and among theologians. The catchword for it: *postmodernity*.

I didn't consciously set myself up to examine this new phenomenon, but it so happened that the seminary I was associated with was paying a very high premium for the freedom of academic inquiry. In addition, California happens to be one of those remarkable laboratories in today's world for generating and testing innovative ideas in one of the most challenging pluralistic cultures I have ever been a part of. The 1980s and '90s were the years of intense probing into the ethical, theological, and philosophical framework of the emerging Anglo-American postmodernity.[5]

Again, it wasn't the intellectual pursuit that was most appealing for me in this exercise, but deep personal relationships and friendships with profound thinkers and committed Christians. By God's grace, some of them were my mentors, helping me to conceptualize the irreversible shift of contemporary culture in society and in the church. Theology, like science, which has been a part of my life for more than 20 years, has the advantage of drawing concepts out of realities. Yet initially I couldn't relate the innovative ideas concerning the current shift and the academic probing into its communal nature to a distinct form of church life. The churches I was acquainted with were functioning as clubs or coping with the memories of the distant past.

As most armchair theologians do, I was looking for a form of church life organized around distinct postmodern principles and doctrines, which was obviously wrong. James McClendon helped me to realize that theology deals with matters much deeper than abstract principles and concepts. The beginning and the end of any meaningful theological reflection is the life of the believing community and its convictions.[6] Yet if theology should necessarily start with the church, should it always be confined to the limits of the church? Glen Stassen guided me through the chemistry of the formation of the person's and community's convictions. This is how I became aware of the power of loyalties, interests, and cultural attachments in tuning our Christian convictions.[7] Finally Nancey Murphy applied a philosophical touch to my intellectual inquiries. She opened my eyes to the epistemological, linguistic, and metaphysical complexity of religious life, including the power of the moral tradition and the formative role of crises in the life of religious communities.[8]

The church's form of life can't be independent of the surrounding culture. It is a simple fact, but it took time for me to fully comprehend it. I began to wonder whether the current crises in Christian communities, both West and East, are necessarily only of dogmatic or doctrinal nature. Could they be seen as an instinctive reaction against the changes in the life of a larger society? Then the fundamentalist turn in the life of the churches, denominations, and seminary communities appeared to be an attempt to preserve intact a status quo formed under the culture of the past against the challenges of changing culture.

Two circumstances helped me sharpen these observations. One was my intimate involvement in the life of the Slavic immigrant communities of the United States. I saw their pain and agony as they tried to preserve, at any cost, the traditional form of life and worship in a completely different culture.

The other was a special event signaling an alternative stance. I recall the meeting of Terra Nova (now called Emergent) in Pasadena, California.[9] A group of young ministers and practical theologians gathered for the purpose of making sense of the same challenges and questions I was struggling with. Well-educated and easily conversing with both the church and academia, they were not merely interested in intellectual sophistication. Unlike many theologians and philosophers still trying to make up their minds about the existence of the phenomenon, they all were, in one way or another, already engaged with postmodernism. Together with other pilgrims, they were working to bring coherence to the life of the church in close proximity to the shifting culture.

My return to Europe about two years ago spurred some further reflection on the predicaments of church life in current culture. By God's strange providence, I was brought to a seminary community that is a stage for theological engagement with the life of 51 national Baptist bodies in Europe, Asia, and the Middle East. This opened up the many faces of post-modernity for me. Most importantly, however, I got away from the North American context, which is largely a product of Enlightenment modernity, in which my confidence had been just shaken. I discovered that different currents have been subverting European modernity for at least 100 years through art, literature, music, and architecture, and which were recently recognized in philosophy and theology.

I also have to admit that Christianity is not the dominant culture of Europe anymore. The Enlightenment project succeeded at least in substituting Christian religion with the religions of secularism and humanism (although, to be sure, even they are Christianized). Post-Christian realities pose a great challenge to Christian formation. The Protestants, the Radicals, the Revivalists of the past had a prophetic say in the still-Christian culture. For something to be protested against, radicalized or revived, it must be there in the first place. Now in many parts of Europe the church has to learn to be a minority, witnessing to the culture that is increasingly secularist and aggressively antireligious.[10] It is a situation yet to be faced by the North American churches.

Like the early Christian communities, the church has to learn the sign language of God's revelation of the newness in Christ in order to make her voice intelligible. In post-something realities, her language should be a holistic language of integrity and care that the cultures can first see and then understand. The best form of theology is theology that is deeply rooted in life itself. A meaningful theology is a practical theology that is engaged with the post-something context. I also see some new avenues for Christian witness. The deep roots of Christianity are still preserved in the beauty and richness of the cultural life of the Western civilization. Christian sentiments can still be recovered more easily through artistic forms than through intellectual artifacts.

These sentiments can catch the rationalistic minds by surprise and open them for dialogue. This dialogue can proceed successfully if the church is living a life that is faithful to her calling and relevant to the culture around her, imparting the Holy Ghost without succumbing to the culture's ghosts.

Questions

1. How effective is the process of being "initiated into faith"? What are some of the limitations and benefits of this process?

2. What other belief systems do we tend to inherit from our families and culture? Why are these so hard to overturn when we have personal revelations that call us to new places?

3. How has the presence of the Holy Ghost in your life caused you to confront some of your previous ideas? How has your life changed as a result?

4. What do you think about faithful moral living for the credibility of our Christian witness? How has that influence changed as the church has emerged?

AFTERWORD

We're Not Finished
Brian D. McLaren

EACH OF THE STORIES YOU'VE READ IS UNIQUE. They don't all follow a single pattern; they don't end up at the same place. But the stories you've read seem to have several things in common.

First, they're stories, not states. So much of our religious language describes the spiritual life as if it were a static state. Even conversion is described, not as a dynamic process, but as an instantaneous passing from one state to another: *I was/got saved/born again/converted. I became a born-again/Reformed/Orthodox/Spirit-filled/victorious/whatever Christian. I was filled/baptized/sanctified in/with/by the Holy Spirit/Ghost.*

True, there are states to be described in the spiritual life—growing, stagnant, dead, alive—as there are in biological life—infancy, childhood, adulthood, death. But these stories of emergence make clear that even within a state such as adulthood, dynamic stories continue.

I remember when this thought hit me, sometime in my 30s: *you never grow up.* Even if you're legally and biologically a certified member of the state of adulthood, you continue to go through many passages (to use Gail Sheehy's useful term)…many dangers, toils, and snares…many frustrations and breakthroughs…many learnings and unlearnings and relearnings. This was a disappointing realization to me, because I had imagined since my junior high years that eventually I would reach the tidy state of adulthood where life would calm down, questions would be finally answered, commitments secure, routines established, beliefs cemented, change complete. Looking back, I had confused adulthood with death, not realizing that adult life is really just an extension of junior high.

You may have come to the same conclusion as you have read these stories: *people, including Christians, never grow up,* which is probably a good thing for those who believe in Someone who places a high value on being childlike and whose favorite words included *follow* and *learn of me* and *repent* (re-think). Our stories never end as long as we're alive. (And even after that, they have a new beginning!)

Some years ago while I was preaching a sermon, having departed from my notes and having further departed from my original tangent into a welter of sub-sub-tangents, I found myself rambling on about the kinds of questions spiritual seekers and new converts have. I offhandedly added, "Of course, the really tough questions are the ones you ask when you've been a Christian for 20 years." My congregation seemed to return to consciousness at this remark, and an audible groan rose spontaneously from nearly everyone (or so it seemed) over 35, a groan of agreement, a sad groan in a way, yet grateful to be acknowledged.

You're an adult reader, but you're still a junior high kid, too, still questioning and learning and unlearning and relearning. The questions you're asking now are probably the toughest and most profound you've ever asked. Your story is ongoing, and changes are possible—no, inevitable. (Even resisting change changes you into a more resistant person, you know?) Perhaps these stories will help you see that you're not abnormal for being 35 or 55 or 75 and still feeling that you're on a journey, in process, unfinished. Rather, you're alive! You're like the 80-something fellow I met in the mountains of Pennsylvania. I asked him, "Have you lived here your whole life?" He answered, "Not yet."

Like the storytellers in this book, you may be emerging from a familiar state where you've long found yourself into a dynamic new story. That can be scary, I know. I hope that, with whatever disappointment or anxiety this realization brings you, it also brings you hope for better days ahead.

Second, these stories reflect a shared discontent with modern evangelicalism. However you want to define the postmodern condition (incredulity toward metanarratives, discontentment with modern civilization, becoming enlightened about the Enlightenment, etc.), it's clear that to be postmodern means to feel that modern culture is (to some degree) on the wrong track, including modern Christianity. Some (like Frederica Mathewes-Green) have escaped the hot, stale, oxygen-poor air of modernity by exploring incense-rich premodern forms of Christianity, while others are seeking to push beyond modern Christianity into unexplored terra nova, cherishing all the resources of premodern Christianity (and modern Christianity, too) while moving on.

For readers who love and identify with modern evangelicalism, who find it satisfying and true and who don't understand this dissatisfaction, these stories could—but shouldn't—be considered a slap in the face, a rejection, a repudiation. You will no doubt feel some frustration and even anger from many people experiencing stories of emergence. But if you interpret those emotions graciously, you will conclude (I believe) that people like the storytellers in this book have come not to bury modern evangelicalism, but to continue it in a new era, under new conditions, in new ways.

A few years ago, William Hendricks (son of evangelical patriarch Howard Hendricks of evangelical mecca Dallas Theological Seminary) published an important—and underappreciated—book entitled *Exit Interviews: Revealing Stories of Why People Are Leaving Church.*[1] Not long after, Mike Regele published *Death of the Church.*[2] These are not happy titles. For those prone to lament or critique the trajectory of the stories in this volume (and the thousands of unpublished stories which parallel them), it's good to remember that we're talking *emergence* here, not *exiting* or *expiring.* The stories in this volume represent an ongoing…no, more than ongoing…*growing* and *passionate* commitment to the Christian faith, to the local church, to the ongoing message and community and revolution begun by Jesus Christ. That's good news!

Perhaps the important questions these stories, with all their status quo discontent, pose for evangelical gatekeepers are these: will the definition of evangelical be flexible enough to include these brothers and sisters as their stories progress or will it snap back to more rigid confines? Will these emerging Christians be included as the *younger evangelicals* (the term Robert Webber uses to describe them[3]) or even as post evangelicals (as David Tomlinson calls them[4]) or will they be excluded and so known as ex-evangelicals?

Put more positively: can the gatekeepers of modern evangelicalism see these brothers and sisters as resources, pioneers, a research-and-development wing of the movement…or will they see them as a threat? That story remains to be told.

Which brings us to the third commonality shared by these stories. These stories are part of a larger untold story, a megastory of change, transition, ferment, and foment, that is still being written, a story bigger than evangelicalism or Protestantism or Christianity or even so-called organized religion. The bigger current in which all these stories flow is a story of our planet, of human beings, of the clash and crash of civilizations, of the waxing and waning of systems of thought and attitudes of mind shared by millions of individuals over generations and across continents in God's unfolding creation.

That larger story is one we can't claim to understand, even though we try. It's too big and grand, and we're too small and short-lived. We wonder, *What's really going on in the megastory, and how do these individual tales fit in with it?* God knows. We don't.

But these storytellers share a common hope that their struggles (which are far from over—remember, we never finish growing up) will be worthwhile, that their reaching and aspiring and seeking and finding and learning/unlearning/relearning will be fruitful, that their stories will somehow advance the story of a mystery articulated by Jesus, a mystery called the kingdom of God, a story of God's will being done on earth as it is in heaven.

The good news in all these stories is that if you feel spiritually stuck, if you find yourself asking crazy new questions, and if you're unsatisfied with the standard answers you're being given…as Spencer Burke notes, "You're not the only crazy one out there."

I remember when I first started asking questions that launch one on an adventure of emergence. I was terrified. Was I losing my faith? My mind? Would I lose my friends? My job?

I had encountered some of the intellectual seeds of postmodernity as a graduate student in literature in the '70s. I sat in a literary criticism seminar one afternoon, discussing Stanley Fish's *Self-Consuming Artifacts*. I remember thinking, "If this guy's ideas catch on, the whole world will change, and Christianity is in a lot of trouble." Twenty years later, I had left academia and had entered the pastorate, and a strange feeling started creeping up my spine: those strange ideas *had* caught on, and the world was changing as a result. That began a dark night for my soul, a time of facing my questions and questioning my faith. Ultimately my questions deconstructed it, leaving me with piles of faith fragments scattered on the floor, wondering if they could ever be reconfigured into a faith that would make sense, a faith that works, a faith that rings true with Scripture and tradition.

Some people can stay isolated in a conservative Christian bubble (of Christian radio, TV, bookstores, schools, theme parks), where they can avoid these kinds of questions and thoughts—and perhaps they can isolate their children as well.

Of those who cannot or will not isolate themselves, some will leave the church as it is and return later to the same churches as they are.

But I consider it highly likely that a large number of people who grow up in our modern churches—evangelical or liberal, Protestant or Catholic—will leave and *never return*—at least, not to our churches as they are.

I do not think it is inevitable that they will never return to the Christian faith. (Many of them will ask, as Peter once did, "Where else can I go? Who else has the words of eternal life?") But I do believe they will only be able to return to the Christian faith when it has reincarnated, if you will, recycled itself, reimagined and rethought and reformed and reexpressed itself for life in the emerging postmodern culture.

This won't simply involve some clever new model of church, some new gimmick, lingo, or style. It will require a metamorphosis far deeper. Whatever the process is that will give birth to the new expression of Christian faith, life, and mission for the emerging culture, it isn't over yet. In fact, it's just beginning, and many of the people whose stories you've now read are pioneers, explorers, and innovators in that process. For this reason, I hope that each reader will sincerely pray for the brothers and sisters you've gotten to know here rather than critiquing or belittling or finding fault.

Like these brothers and sisters, you may have a story of emergence that you'd like to make available to others. If so, please go to www.emergentYS.com, where you'll find a place to post your story. In this way, this book will become an introduction to a much longer work in progress that readers like yourself will help create. The multiplying of stories will help create more safe space for people to talk about their questionings, wonderings, and emergings.

You can also create safe space by bringing some friends together and reading this book as a group. Each time you meet, read a story and share where it resonates with your own.

As you share your own story and others, remember that even though we're all adults, none of us is finished yet. For that reason, each chapter in this book should end with the words *to be continued*, and so should this book itself.

To be continued…

ENDNOTES

Mike Yaconelli

1. *In the Name of Jesus* by Henri J. M. Nouwen, (Crossroad/Herder & Herder, 1993).

2. Please understand, I'm making generalizations here. On many Sundays the only fragrance is grumpiness or pettiness or depression. Those things happen, but, in general, on an average, somehow the grace of God manages to show up even then.

Jo-Ann Badley

No notes

Jay Bakker

1. Isaiah 42:2-3.

George R. Baum

1. At the time of this conversation, Karl was on the verge of escaping the faith of his childhood. In his case, he had a completely different set of issues to work through than my Lutheran upbringing gave to me. Karl later apologized for having been so forceful about this, explaining that folks tend to most strongly argue theories just when they're on the verge of abandoning those beliefs.

Spencer Burke

1. *The Cloud of Unknowing*, translated by William Johnston (Image Books, 1996); *The Dark Night of the Soul* by St. John of the Cross (Image Books, 1959); *Wisdom of the Desert* by Thomas Merton, (New York: Norton, 1988).

2. *The Road Not Taken* by Robert Frost (New York: Henry Holt, 1985).

Brad Cecil

1. *The Web of Belief* by W.V. Quine; second edition (McGraw Hill, Inc., 1978).

2. *Philosophical Investigations* (third edition) by Ludwig Wittgenstein, translated by G.E.M Anscombe (Prentice Hall, 1999).

3. *Evangelicalism & The Future of Christianity* by Alister McGrath (InterVarsity Press, 1995).

4. Here's my list of modern (Enlightenment) tools:

- *Foundationalism*. We can find an irreducible starting point to build all knowledge upon.

- *Sufficiency of Language*. Language is pure and without cultural bias.

- *Objectivity*. Truth resides in the objects of the world and is without interpretation.

- *Rationalism*. All rational individuals have the same interpretation.

- *Empiricism*. We can trust what we validate with empirical senses (sight, sound, smell, etc.).

- *Certainty*. We can find a place of no doubt.

- *Truth*. The way things really are.

- *Universalism*. The quest to find truths that are undeniable to all of the universe.

- *Absolutism*. We can obtain a complete, accurate, pure understanding of reality.

Here's my list of postmodern tools:

- *Web*. Our knowledge is built within an intricate web of concepts, language, relationships, and experiences and is always changing.

- *Cultural Linguistic*. Language is tied closely to the concepts embraced in a culture, and it is not pure.

- *Pluralism*. All individuals have a unique and varying understanding of the reality of the world.

- *Empirical Mysticism*. There is more to the world than what can be validated by our senses.

- *Contingency*. All we understand and know is contingent upon many things and what we believe, we believe with prior assumptions.

- *Truth*. What we call truth is actually an agreement formed within a cultural setting.

- *Limitations*. We have begun to understand the significant limitations of language, concepts, culture, and understanding, which prevents us from obtaining complete understanding.

5. *Texts Under Negotiation: The Bible and Postmodern Imagination* by Walter Brueggeman (Augsburg Fortress Press, 1993).

6. Taken from an address given at the Religion and Postmodernity Conference, published in *God, the Gift, and Postmodernism* by John D. Caputo and Michael J. Scanlon (eds.) (Indiana University Press, 1999).

7. Brueggeman.

Earl Creps

1. If only this metaphor were original to me. I picked it up in one of many field interviews with emerging church leaders. My best recollection is that it came from Barry Taylor, pastor of New Ground in West Hollywood, California.

2. *Calling* by Rich Hurst and Frank Tillapaugh (Dreamtime, 1997), 48-53.

3. *The Third Wave of the Holy Spirit* by C. Peter Wagner, (Vine Books, 1988), 29-35, 75-86.

4. Wagner, 16-18.

5. *The Church on the Other Side* by Brian D. McLaren (Zondervan, 2000).

6. Thanks to Len Sweet for so many illuminating metaphors, including those of water and fluidity developed in books such as *AquaChurch* (Group, 1995) and *SoulTsunami* (Zondervan, 1999) and the citizenship image he paints in *Carpe Mañana* (Zondervan, 2001). Len is doing for the emerging church what Carl Sagan did for astrophysics.

7. *Carpe Mañana*

James F. Engel

1. *The Scandal of the Evangelical Mind* by Mark Noll (Eerdmans, 1994).

2. Noll, 42.

3. *The Revival of 1857-1858: Interpreting an American Religious Awakening* by Kathryn T. Long (Oxford University Press, 1997).

4. This is the position taken by John Bunyan in *Pilgrim's Progress*. You may find it helpful to read this wonderful classic in modern English. See *Pilgrim's Progress in Today's English* retold by James H. Thomas (Moody Press, 1964). Current thinking on the Engel scale is presented in *Changing the Mind of Missions* by James F. Engel and William A. Dyrness (InterVarsity Press, 2000), chapter 4.

5. *More Ready Than You Realize* by Brian D. McLaren (Zondervan, 2002).

6. *What's Gone Wrong with the Harvest?* by James F. Engel and H. Wilbert Norton, (Zondervan, 1975).

7. *Changing the Mind of Missions*.

8. John Wesley, quoted in *The Radical Wesley* by Howard A. Snyder (InterVarsity Press, 1983), 85.

9. *The Spontaneous Expansion of the Church and Missionary Methods* by Roland Allen (Wipf & Stock Pub., 1997) (Eerdmans, 1962).

Todd Hunter

1. *Sex, Economy, Freedom & Community* by Wendell Berry (Pantheon, 1994), xix.

2. *Beyond Foundationalism* by Stanley Grenz and John Franke (John Knox, 2000), 253.

3. "Living into God's Story" by Eugene Peterson, retrieved from www.theooze.com/articles on June 7, 2002.

4. *The Message* by Eugene Peterson (NavPress, 2002).

5. See the Parable of the Hidden Treasure and the Parable of the Pearl in Matthew 13:44-46.

6. See The Parable of the Tenants in Matthew 21:33-41.

7. *Mind, Language and Society* by John R. Searle (Basic, 1998), 39.

8. Searle, 14.

9. *The New Testament and the People of God* by N. T. Wright, (Fortress, 1996), 32-46.

Tony Jones

1. By writing these paragraphs in the past tense, I don't mean to suggest that this movement has abated or that these church planters are less engaged with culture than they were. I only mean to write about my own experience as these ideas began to dawn on me and to, in some way, bring you back there with me.

Frederica Mathewes-Green

1. *Fire with Fire* by Naomi Wolf (Random House, 1993).

Parush R. Parushev

1. On John Meyendorff, Alexander Schmemann, and Gerges Florovsky as contemporary church Fathers of the Orthodox community see *New Perspectives on Historical Theology: Essays in Memory of John Meyendorff* by Bradley Nassif (ed) (Eerdmans, 1996), xvi.

2. Recorded in "On Methods and Means in Theology" by Harold O. J. Brown in *Doing Theology in Today's World: Essays in Honor of Kenneth S. Kantzer,* edited by John D. Woodbridge and Thomas Edward McComskey (Zondervan, 1991), 147-69.

3. Coming from a completely different perspective Asen Ignatov—a well-known political scientist—argues also for the irrational nature of the Communist system of beliefs in *Psychologie des Kommunismus* (Iohanes Bergmans Verlag, 1985).

4. On the danger of the abuse of power in the church see *Ethics: Systematic Theology, Volume I,* James Wm. McClendon, Jr. (Abingdon, 1896), 173-77.

5. "Distinguishing Modern and Postmodern Theologies" by Nancey Murphy and James Wm McClendon, Jr. in *Modern Theology* 5:3 (April): 145-68.

6. *Convictions: Defusing Religious Relativism* by James Wm. McClendon,Jr. and James M. Smith (Trinity Press, 1994).

7. *Authentic Transformation: A New Vision of Christ and Culture* by Glen H. Stassen, D.M. Yeager, and John Howard Yoder (Abingdon, 1996) and "A Social Theory Model for Religious Social Ethics" by Glen H. Stassen in *Journal of Religious Ethics* 5 (1977): 9-37.

8. *Anglo-American Postmodernity: Philosophical Perspectives on Science, Religion, and Ethics* by Nancey Murphy (Westview Press, 1997) and "Epistemological Crises, Dramatic Narrative, and the Philosophy of Science" by Alasdair MacIntyre in *The Monist* 60 (1977): 453-72.

9. Thanks to Andrew Jones and Brian McLaren for the invitation, and to the participants in the Terra Nova Dialogue (January 08-10, 2001) for the encouragement and insights.

10. An excellent book on the subject is *New Baptist, New Agenda* by Nigel G. Wright (Paternoster, 2002).

Chris Seay

1. "Postmodernity," by Mark Driscoll, posted at www.marshill.fm/content_2000_q3/kairos/culture/postmodernity_view.htm on September 30, 2002.

Chuck Smith, jr.

1. *Cultural Anthropology* by Stephen A. Grunlan and Marvin Keene Mayers (Zondervan, 1988).

2. *Christianity in Culture* by Chuck Kraft (Orbis, 1979).

3. Europeans generally have a different notion of what constitutes an "evangelical." For many of them, evangelicalism began with the Reformation. What I am referring to is a more recent phenomenon that is especially North American—

though not unique to the U.S. Many histories are available of fundamentalism and evangelicalism by able authors such as George Marsden, Bernard Ramm, and Martin Marty.

Brian D. McLaren

1. *Exit Interviews: Revealing Stories of Why People Are Leaving Church* by William Hendricks (Moody Press, 1993).

2. *Death of the Church* by Mike Regele (Zondervan, 1996).

3. *The Younger Evangelicals* by Robert Webber (Baker, 2002).

4. *The Post Evangelical* by Dave Tomlinson (emergentYS, 2003).